JERALD SIMON

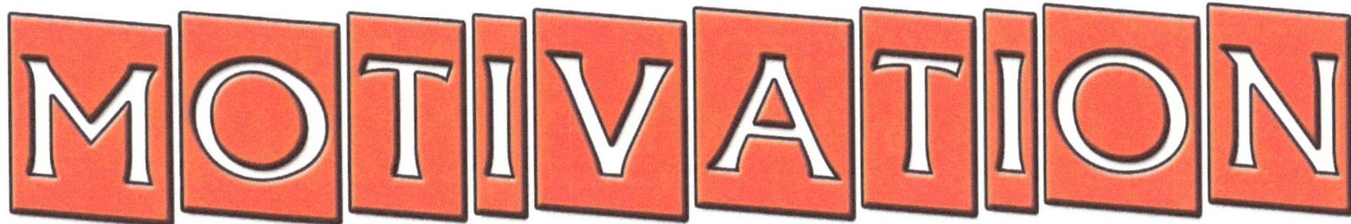

MOTIVATION IN A MINUTE

(BOOK 1)

MUSIC MENTOR

JERALD SIMON

Music Motivation®

Cool music that excites, entertains, and educates!

visit **http://musicmotivation.com**
follow Jerald on Facebook: https://facebook.com/jeraldsimon
subscribe to Jerald's YouTube page: https://youtube.com/jeraldsimon

Innovative Motivation books, published by **Music Motivation®**, are designed to motivate and inspire others with poems, stories, images, and photos that convey an inspirational and motivational message to help them discover their purpose and mission in life. **Smile and be happy!** The author and publisher disclaim any liability or accountability for the misuse of this material as it was intended by the author.

MOTIVATION IN A MINUTE
by JERALD SIMON

Music Motivation®, **http://musicmotivation.com**
P.O. Box 1000 Kaysville, UT 84037-1000 U.S.A.
info@musicmotivation.com; +1-801-444-5143

For more promotional excerpt permission, contact:
Music Motivation®
P.O. Box 1000 Kaysville, UT 84037-1000
http://musicmotivation.com
info@musicmotivation.com

International Standard Book Numbers (ISBN)
Paperback - 978-0-9980785-4-0
eBook - 978-0-9980785-7-1
Audio Book Bar code - 191924274407
Library of Congress Control Number: 2017913302

Printed in the **United States of America**
Simon, Jerald
Jerald Simon's Motivation in a Minute Jerald Simon
Edited by Suzanne Simon and Wendy Cederlof

Welcome to Motivation in a Minute!

In this book I have included short motivational messages with images to inspire individuals of all ages to *do* and *be* their best.

What is your personal mission in life? Have you ever thought about that before? Everyone has something they alone can do, provide, give, teach, share, and pass along to mankind. Some refer to it as leaving a legacy for future generations. Others speak about doing good and serving others by giving back to the community. All of these are correct. It is about discovering and finding out what you would like to focus on throughout your life. It is more than having a mere vocation. It is a calling, a purpose, a passion, a privilege.

Here is what I feel my personal mission in life is:

"My purpose and mission in life is to motivate myself and others through my music and writing, to help others find their purpose and mission in life, and to teach values that encourage everyone everywhere to do and be their best."

Jerald Simon

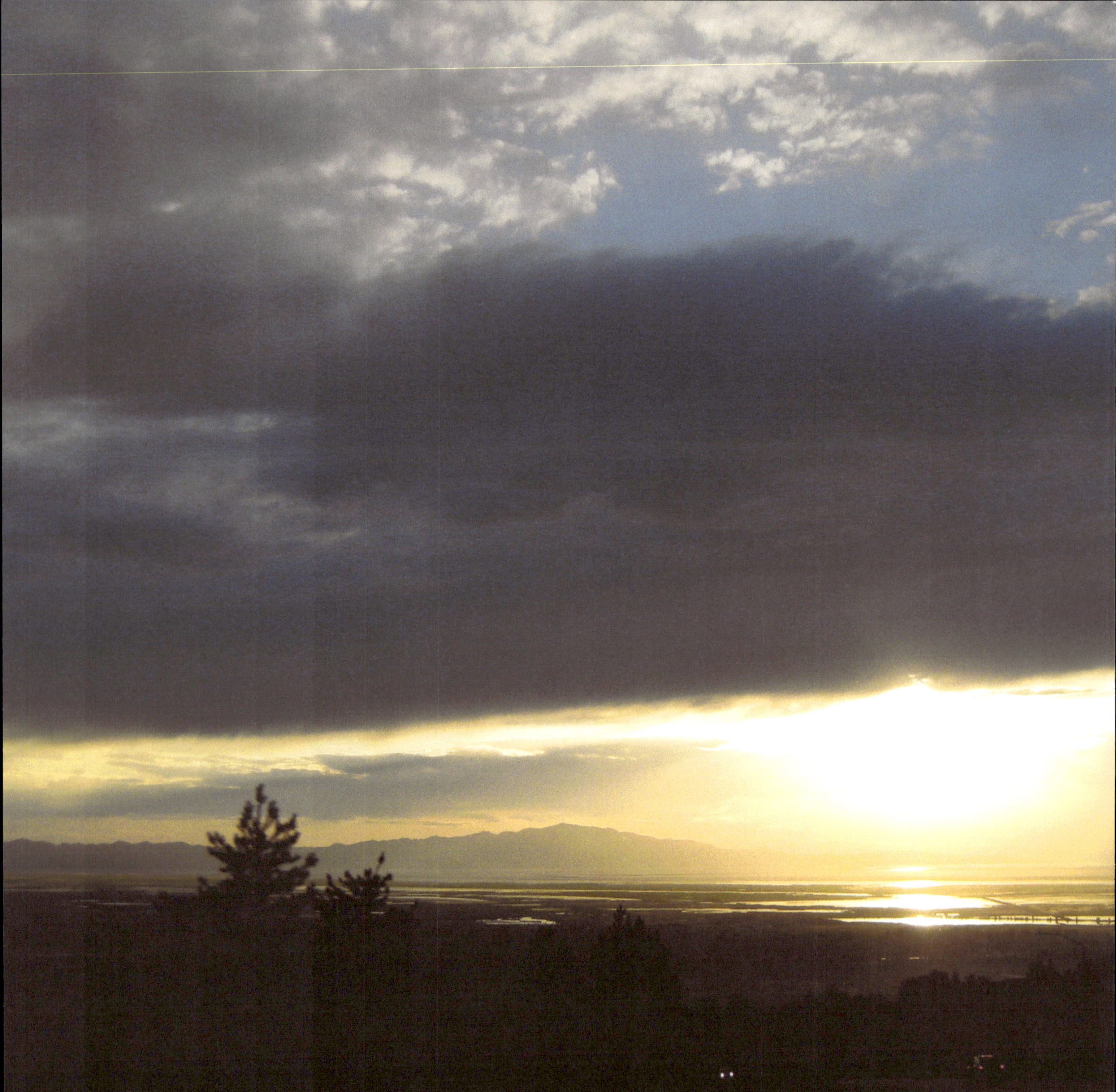

Make it a goal to make goals!

One of the first steps toward accomplishment is knowing what you want to accomplish. You don't need to know every little detail that needs to be done, but you should have a general idea of where you are going. First know where you are and then decide where you would like to end up after everything is said and done.

Plans do change, often very quickly, and you won't always be able to accomplish absolutely everything on your to-do list, and that's okay. This should not stop you from doing everything you can to create one in the first place. Make a to-do list and start following it!

Here are some ideas:

- Write down a list of 5 goals to be accomplished today.
- Write down a list of 5 goals to be accomplished this year.
- Write down a list of 5 new talents you would like to develop.
- Write down 5 new skills you would like to learn this year.
- Write down a paragraph of positivity that you will read each day (morning or night) to help you focus on what matters most.

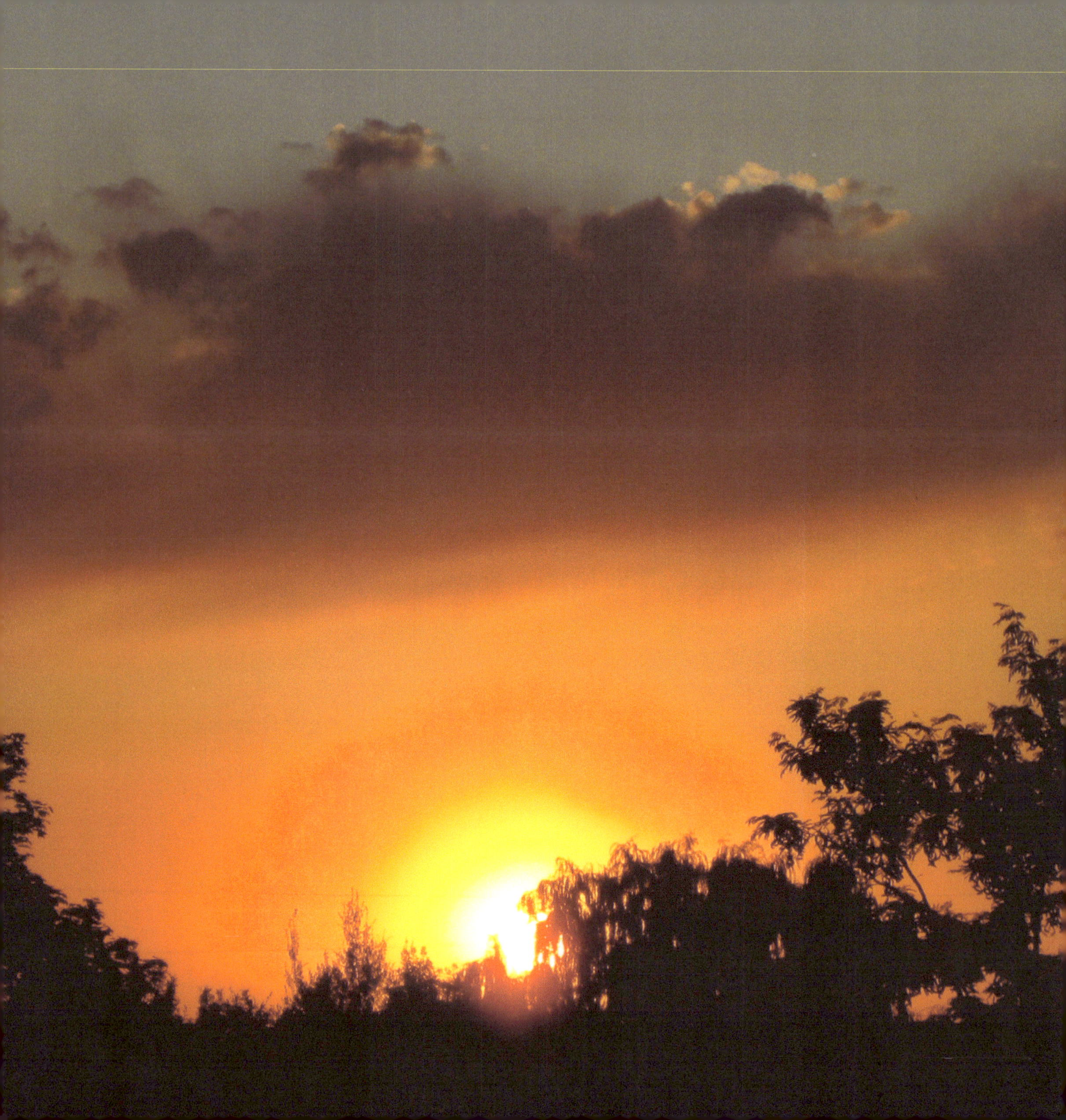

Never ever give up!

Each day is a new day to overcome the mistakes of yesterday. We can learn so much from our first, second, seventh and even 700th attempt at something. We can always learn something new and become our own success story.

There is hope in overcoming our perceived failures. We are successful when we decide to do something we want to do and then follow through with our plans.

Here are some ideas to think about:

- How can you create a personal road map for your future?
- What have you always dreamed of doing but have never done?
- What is one dream destination you'd like to visit this year?
- What new hobby or skill would you like to learn this year?
- How can you finish what you start and continually motivate yourself to keep going even through the tough times?

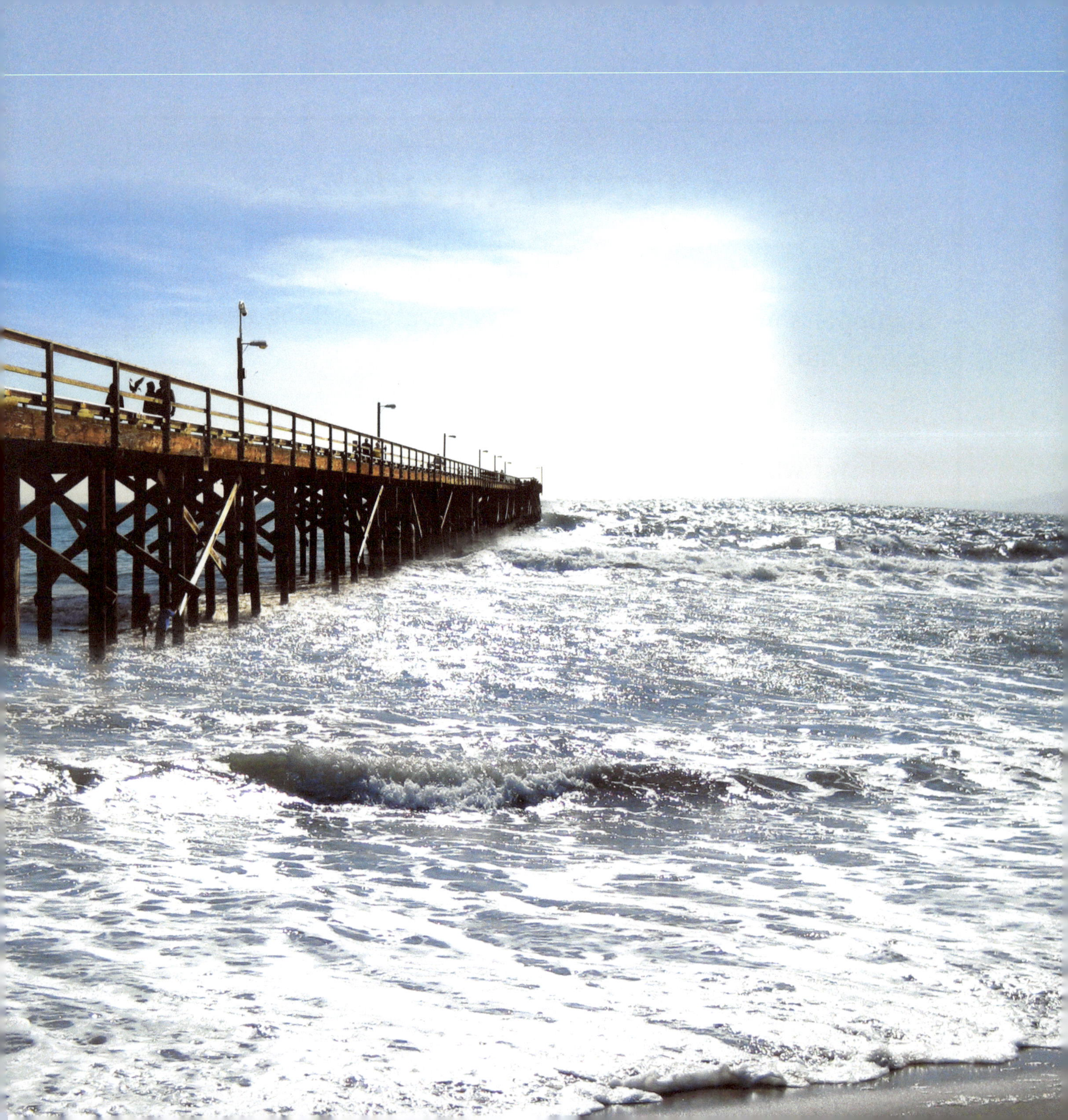

You are the BEST, but always be better!

We must strive to be the absolute best we can be in our particular field, talent, or area of expertise. This is a good goal to motivate us and help us improve and want to be better. We must be *our* best and strive to be better than who we were yesterday. We should try to focus on competing against our personal best and striving to out do what we have done before. Hopefully we want everyone to succeed and do their best. When we help others improve and do better we feel better about ourselves. Success should not be for a select few. Everyone deserves success and to be their best.

Too often we think we are failures because we compare ourselves to others and what they have accomplished. Their successes can help us be more motivated to do our best, but we must not let their strengths and abilities weaken our view of ourselves. We must be inspired by others and try to inspire ourselves to be *our* best.

- How can you be your best in your field or area of expertise?
- How can you help others improve and be their best?

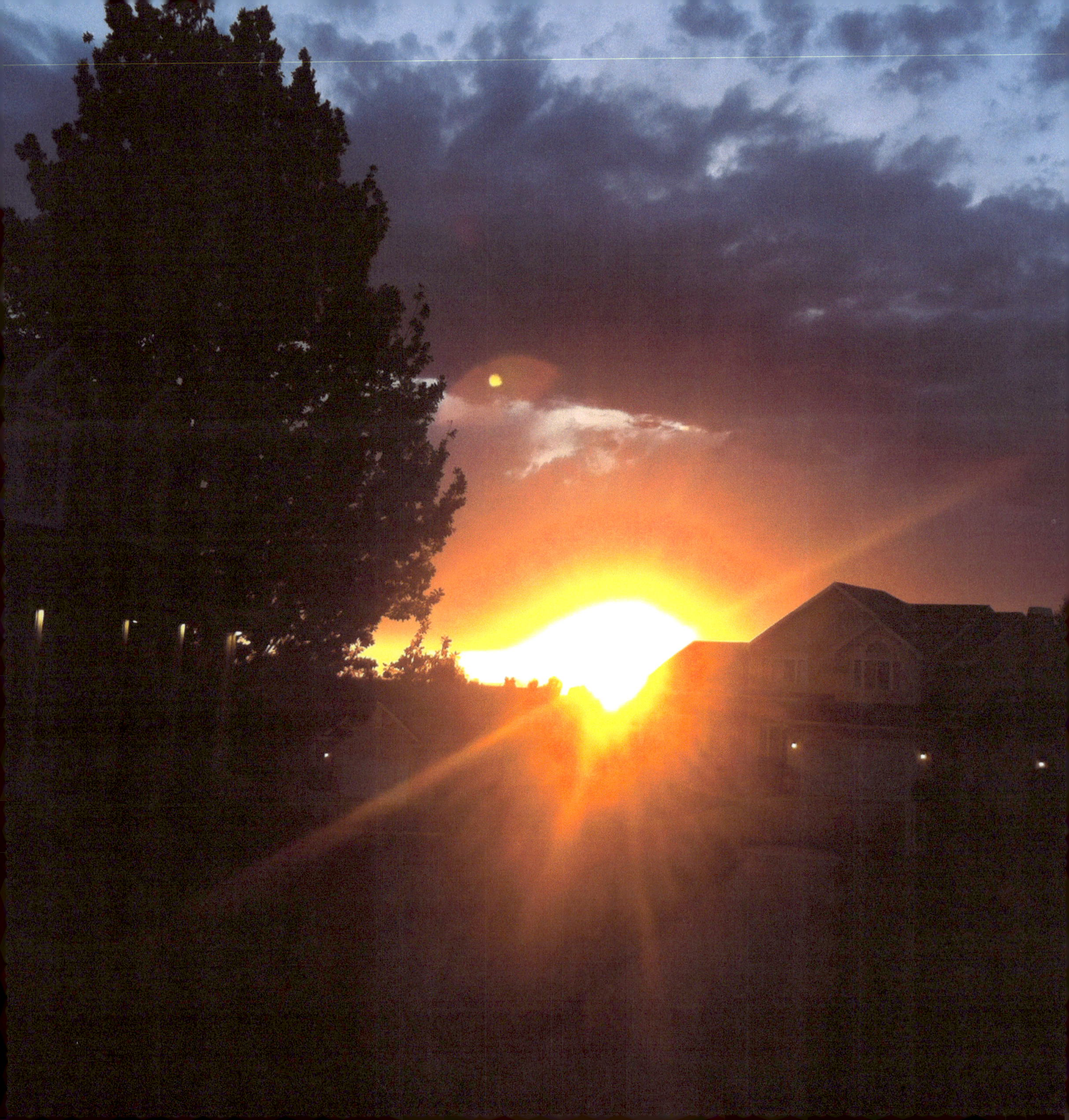

Your time is extremely important!

Every day is a gift from God that we have been given to bless our lives, and also that we might be a blessing to others. That is why we call today the *present*. It is God's gift to us. Live today! Love today!

What would you do differently with your day if you were allowed to create the *perfect* day? This is your chance to imagine what you would like to do hour by hour and minute by minute.

- What does your perfect day look like?
- Who are you with on your perfect day?
- What activities are you doing on your perfect day?
- What can you do to improve your day?
- Now that you have imagined your perfect day, find out what a perfect day looks like for your spouse, your children, family, friends, neighbors, co-workers, etc.. Help them find *their* day.
- What can you do to improve someone else's day?
- How can you help create a perfect day for yourself and others?
- What will you start doing to make today better? How?
- What will you stop doing to make today better? How?

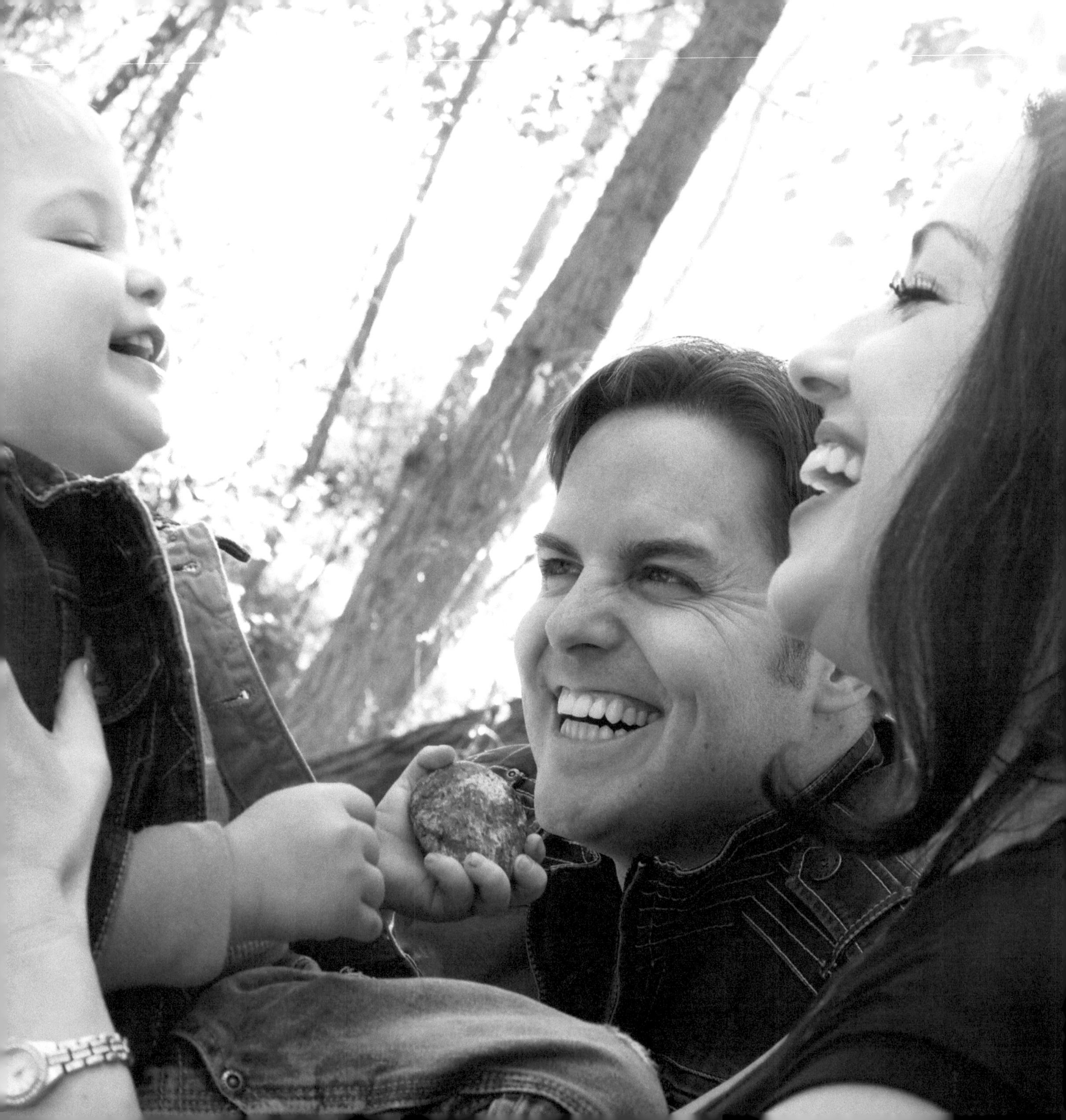

Bring Joy to the World!

Today is a miracle! We should look for the good in every day. At times we all can get frustrated, upset, and even angry at the daily problems in our lives. That is completely understandable and is normal. Everyone has tough times and we all have had painful problems that keep us awake at night. It is a part of life that we must face on a daily basis. We have ups and downs.

That being said, we have a choice we can make each day, hour, and minute of our lives in how we handle these ups and downs. The question is: "Will we react in anger or love?" This applies to every situation, every problem, and every good and bad event in our lives whether or not we initially caused the problem.

If we will find joy in life, we will delight in the simple as well as the profound. Our children can bring us so much joy and we must do our best to focus on that. Yes, there may be times when we are frustrated, but we must never react with anger, unkindness, or do anything that would make others, especially our little ones, sad, hurt, or afraid.

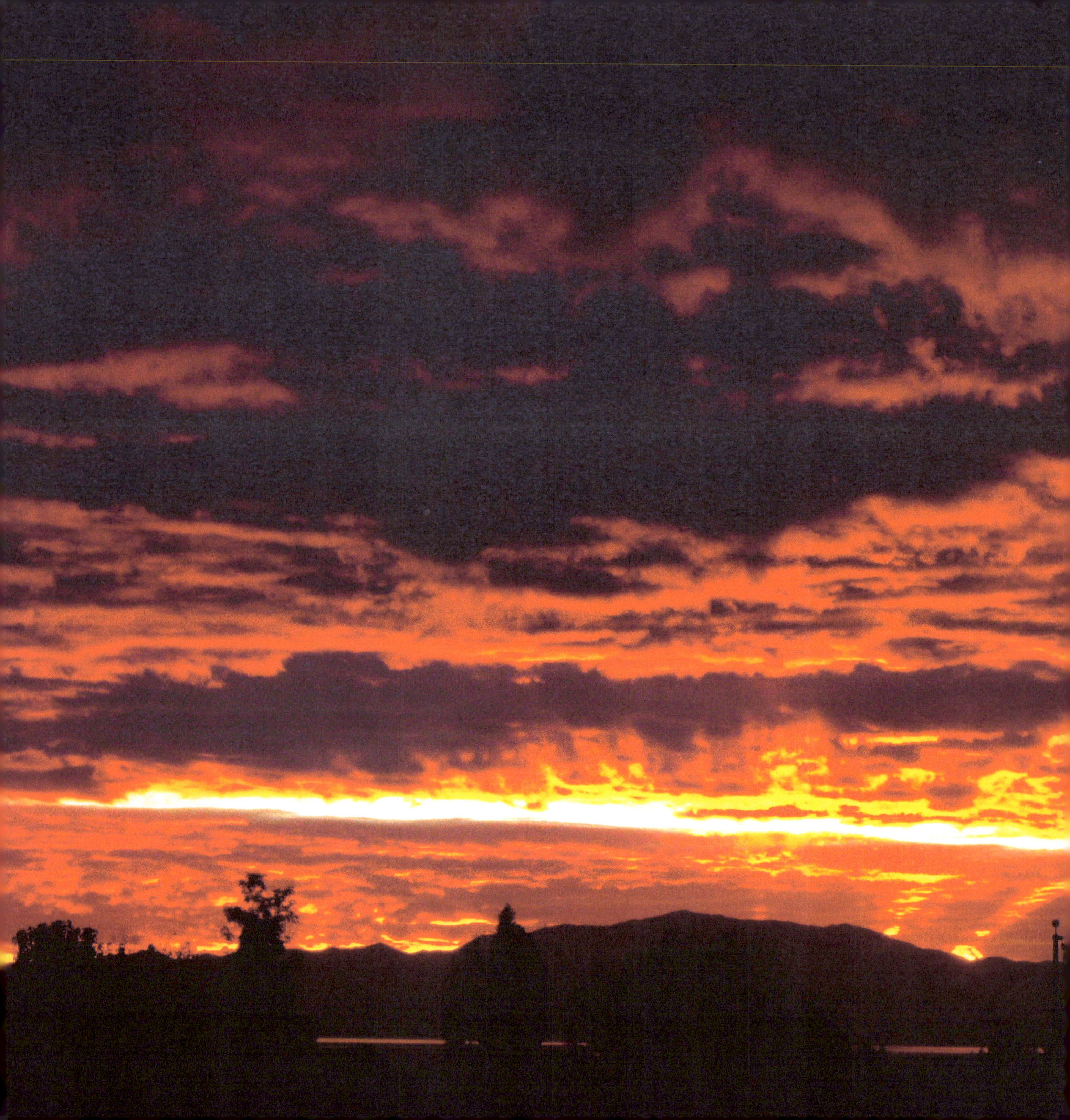

Be thankful each day!

Thank you! That simple two-word phrase can do more to build bridges and mend broken fences than any other epic story could. We could also include "please," "I'm sorry," "forgive me," and "I love you" to that list as well. The words I LOVE YOU are some of the most powerful and healing phrases anyone could ever utter or hope to hear spoken to them. Those words are pure and sacred.

How often do you sincerely thank others? How often do you thank your spouse for everything he/she does for you? How often do you thank your children? Your parents? Your extended family and friends? How often do you thank your neighbors for being there and being wonderful (even if sometimes they are not)?

In order for us to truly appreciate what we have and not take any of these treasures for granted, we must express our gratitude on a daily basis. We must not only show how thankful we are, we must verbalize it and say these life changing words and phrases. Today, say: "Thank you!," "Please," "I'm sorry," "Forgive Me," and "I love you" as often as you can. It will change how you act and behave!

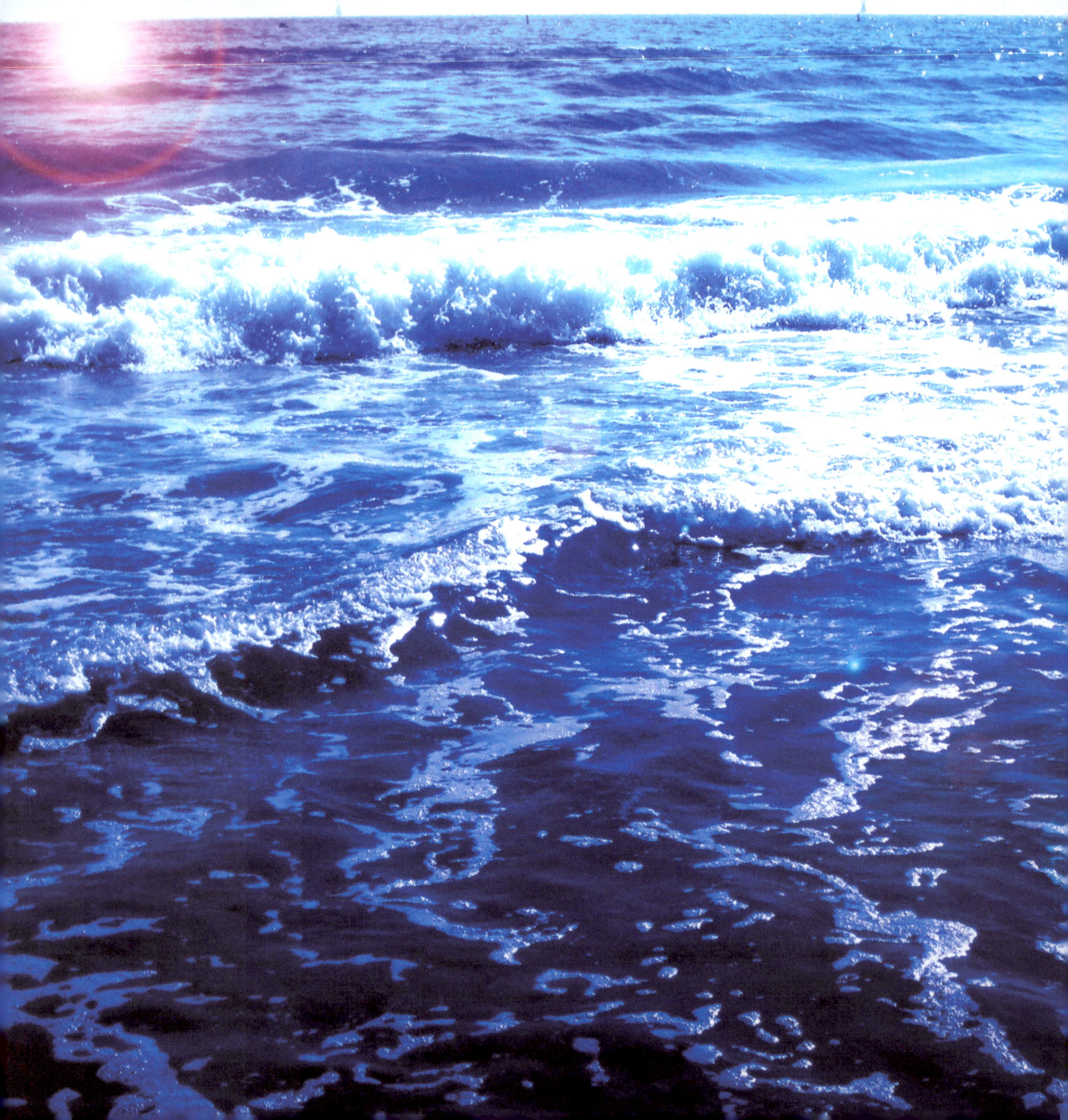

Your Adventure Awaits!

What are you waiting for? When you awoke today, you began a great and glorious journey. Today is the most important day you will ever live. This is your best time to do and be your best! Don't look forward in fear or ponder about past trials or triumphs. Know that today is the most important moment you have. Seize this day! Plan out your day carefully and make the most of each minute. You cannot squander away any second you have, because you have the opportunity to make today and each new day the very best day you have ever had in your life. Live your life to the fullest!

Today is an adventure and you are the tour guide. No one else can live your day for you. It's yours! No one else has your strength for the struggles you face. You are in charge of your thoughts, your feelings, your words, your actions, your successes, and also your failings. You are responsible for you and no one else has that privilege or power. Set sail on an adventure to success!

Make today count!

Get up and get moving!

Some have referred to life as an intense roller coaster ride with its many ups and downs, twists and turns, and stops and starts. Life is completely unexpected, and we never know what will happen each day. One minute we're up and living the high life and the next we are experiencing serious setbacks. The key is to always live life to the fullest. Yes, there are enough sad stories to keep us all awake at night fretting and worrying about the dark days ahead or the calamities that may come. There have always been hiccups on the road that leads to a rewarding life. But with the good and the bad that can come upon us, we can always enjoy the ride! It's the ride of a lifetime and it is our life and our time!

Would you rather dance your way through each day because you are anxiously anticipating what new experiences you will face? Or do you want to be agitated and on edge because you are angry at the world? The choice is yours. Choose to enjoy every minute you have. Live life to the fullest! Enjoy the ride!

The light will come!

Storms have a nasty way of surprising us when we least expect them. Mother Nature's weather patterns can be unreliable and unpredictable!

Sometimes we are so caught up in what is happening around us that we forget we can control our personal weather worries and predict sunnier times by chasing away those cloudy days and allowing the sunshine of sweetness to help us spread smiles wherever we go.

We all have dark days and no one should ever repress their sad feelings. Doing so creates currents of coming calamities. It isn't about spreading syrupy sunshine that reeks of insincerity or pretending to portray peace and serenity at all times. You must be real. The dark storms that swell within people can often be released at the most upsetting and difficult times. Look to the light and extend a hand of hope to everyone. There is always light after every dark storm!

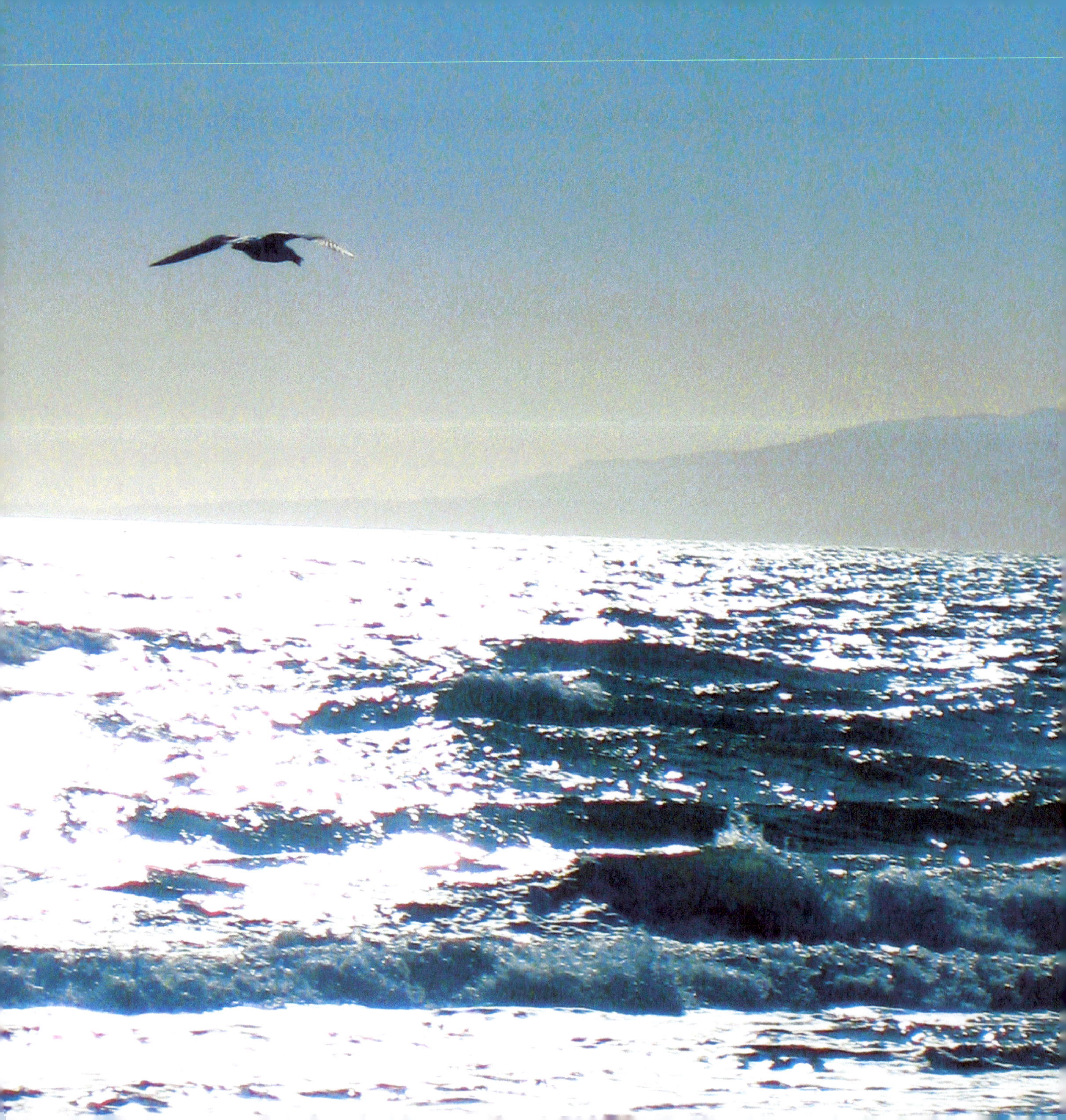

Do your best until you become better!

Far too often we compare ourselves with others. We see our own weaknesses and failures staring at us every time we look into a mirror. We then look at others and compare our weaknesses and failures with their strengths and successes. We may feel we don't measure up because everyone else appears to have it easy! This comparison can be dangerous. If we compare ourselves to others' affluent lifestyles, we can sometimes feel saddened by the peanuts we bring home from our hourly or salary work. This form of comparison comes because we are told from an early age that we must be successful and we are conditioned to get the highest level of education so we can get the best jobs or careers with the highest paid salaries so we can proclaim we have arrived and have succeeded. But have we? Do we? Success is personal. It's different for everyone! It's okay if you don't have everything figured out yet. No one truly does. You'll get there. We all will.

Coast and then soar.

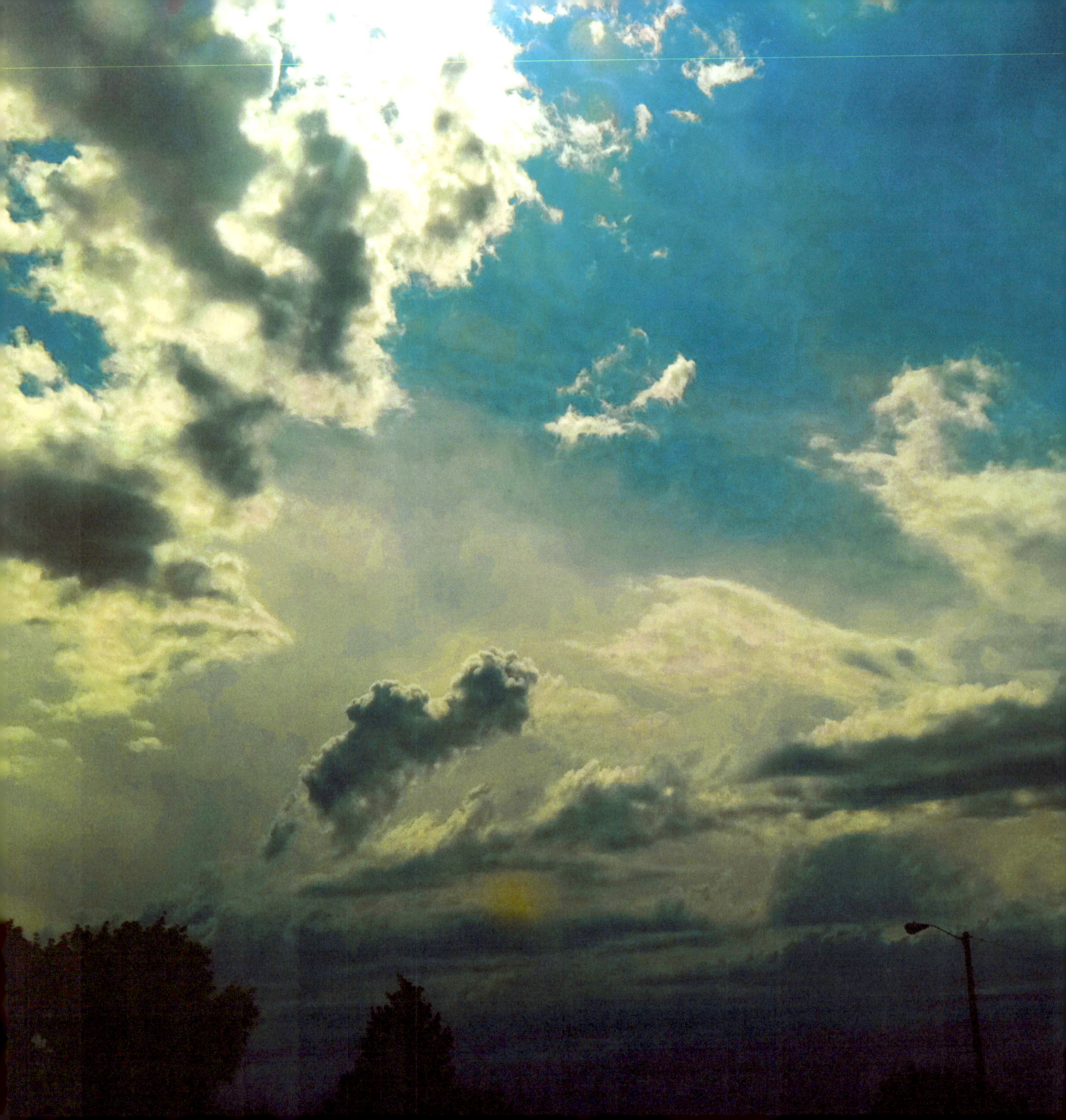

God continually gives us gifts of love!

Do you love yourself? Not in a self-consumed or narcissistic way, but in a humble expression of gratitude to God? You are the workmanship of His love. He loves you unconditionally, and even though you may feel undeserving of His love, He continually gives you everything He knows you need.

Each day is a gift from God. Have you ever looked at the sky and felt a deep appreciation for His gifts of love? You can notice His artwork in everything that surrounds you. See it in a sunset or soak it in during a sunrise. Every cloud in the sky is an example of God's artistic brush strokes. He is the Master artist. You can see His love for you everywhere.

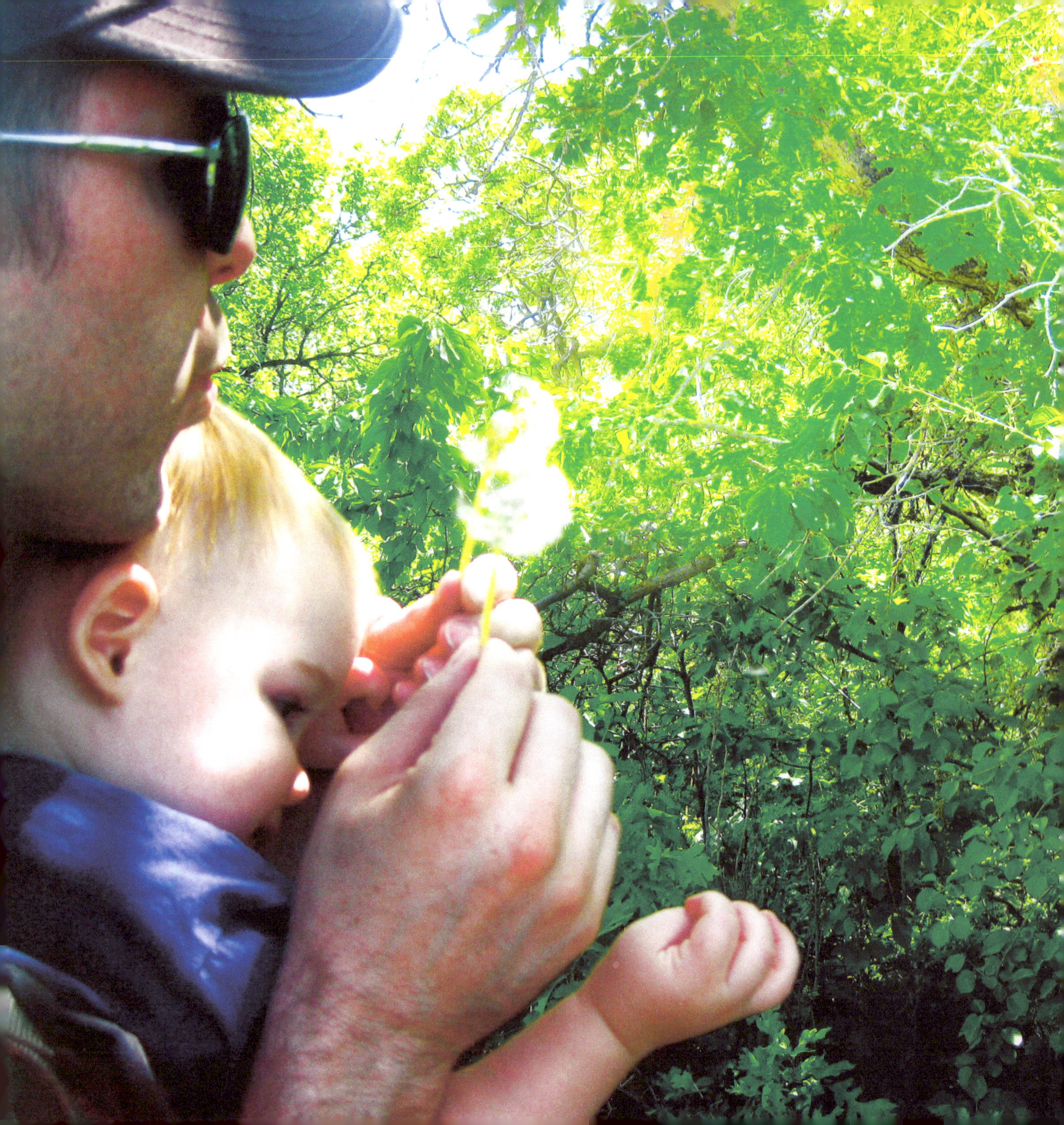

Never stop learning!

Children are the perfect example of falling down, picking themselves up, trying to do the same activity over and over again, and learning something new every day. Children dream, play, and learn, and inspire the rest of us to never grow up.

We are all children at heart. We're just big kids who have grown a little taller!

Never stop asking questions and being inquisitive.

We all can learn from books, courses, teachers, mentors, friends, and relatives. There is a sea of scholars around us who can teach us as we sit at their feet or read their wise and wonderful words of wisdom.

Think of the books found in libraries. Think of the infinite resources available from technology, the Internet, and all of the continually expanding educational formats around the world. We have a world-wide resource available to us at all times. Learn!

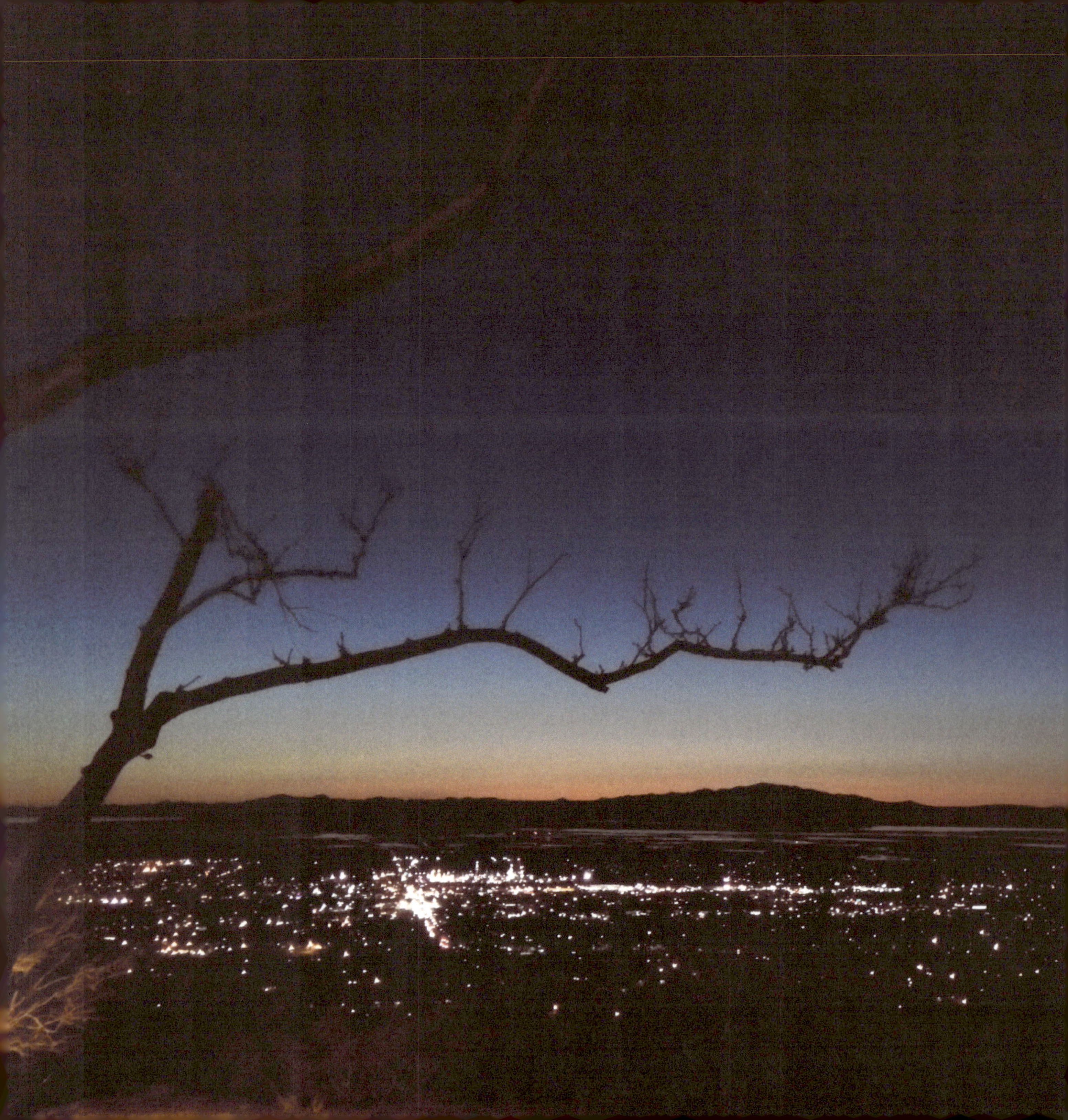

Your future is coming!

The past, present, and future are extremely powerful forces. Far too many of us spend too much time in the past. Others frolic for fun in the future as if it were certain. Both are unsound and unstable. We must always remain in the present.

I often refer to the past as "Parley Past" and the future as "Future Frank". Parley Past is the fellow who lives in the past. Everything he does and says is a salute to the glory days of yesteryear. He remembers, and, sadly, almost idolizes the better times of the past. Individuals like Parley Past reminisce about what they did and could do when they were younger, how much better everything was during simpler times, and how wonderful everything used to be. These people are imprisoned in their past.

Those who fancy the future are always looking forward to better times. They escape their present condition to daydream and see a new and improved version of themselves. They are not present and cannot be. Look to the future in faith, but always be present today!

How well do you know yourself?

Here are some questions to help you get to know yourself a little bit better. Sit down and have a heart to heart talk with the one who stares at you every time you look in a mirror.

Why did you get up today?
What do you hope to accomplish today?
What is the most important item on your to-do list today?
What is the least important activity you are doing today?
Why are you spending so much time doing what you are doing?
If money were not an issue, what would you be doing with your time and with your life? How would things change from the way they are today?
What do you want to change about your current situation in life?
What are your immediate goals for today, tomorrow, and this week? What about this month? What about this year? Next year?
What do you need to change right now to improve the quality of your life? How can you take steps today to eliminate unwanted activities, behaviors, attitudes, words you use but would like not to, etc.? How can you change and be a better version of you?

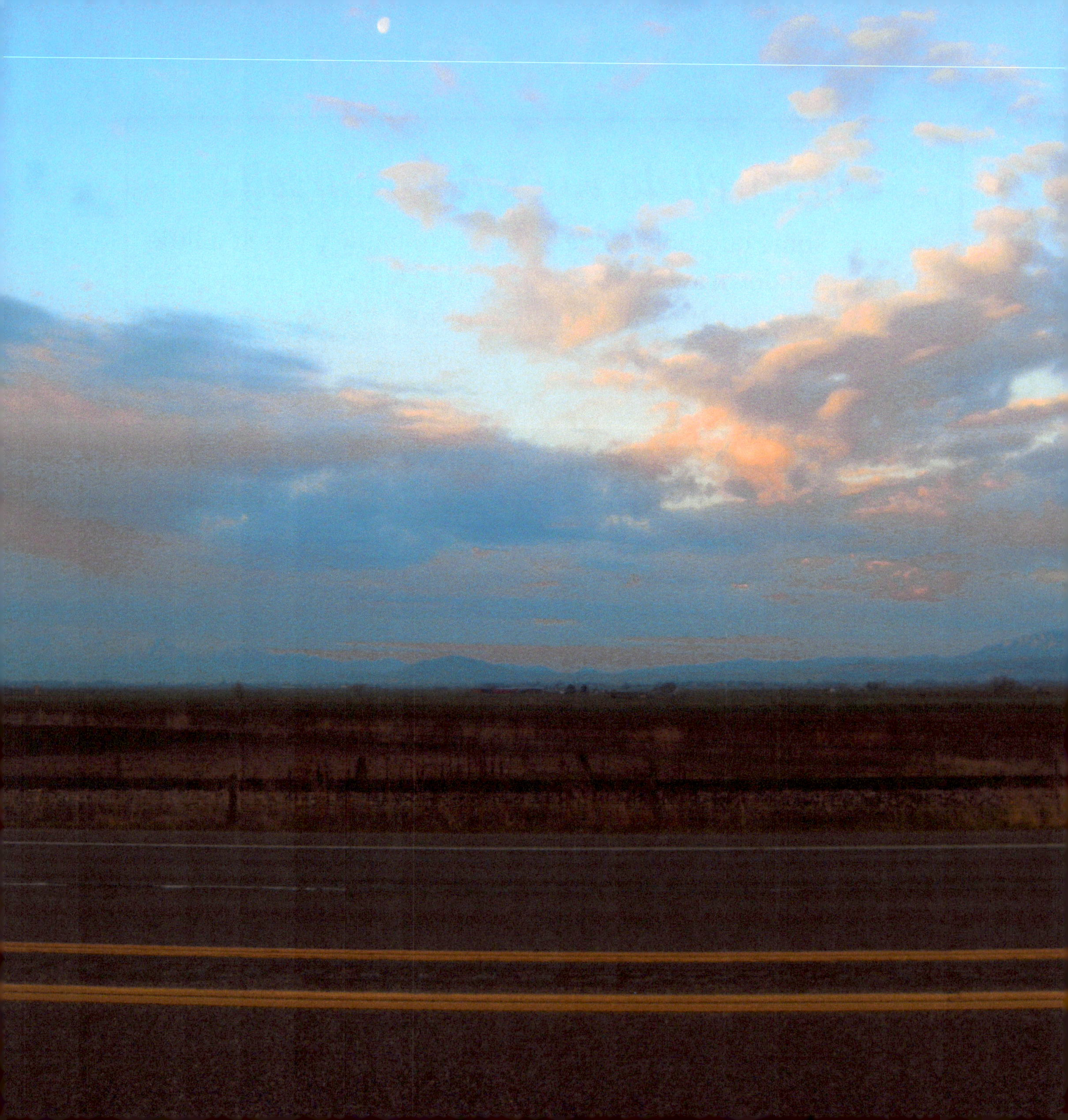

Are you truly living life to the fullest?

What does that statement mean? It means something that is different and unique to everyone because each of us has our own individual needs and circumstances. Right now, are you living your life to your fullest potential? Are you doing what you want to be doing? Are you waking up each morning excited to greet each new day and face the challenges that come your way because you know you are doing what you know you were born to do? If not, what can you do to change things?

Here is another question for you. Are you experiencing your absolute best quality of life because you are learning and growing and using your talents to enrich the lives of others?

All of these questions are difficult to answer and leave most of us feeling a little guilty. There is no need to feel that way, though. We all know we could and should do a bit better. Know where you want to go. ***Live life and love it!***

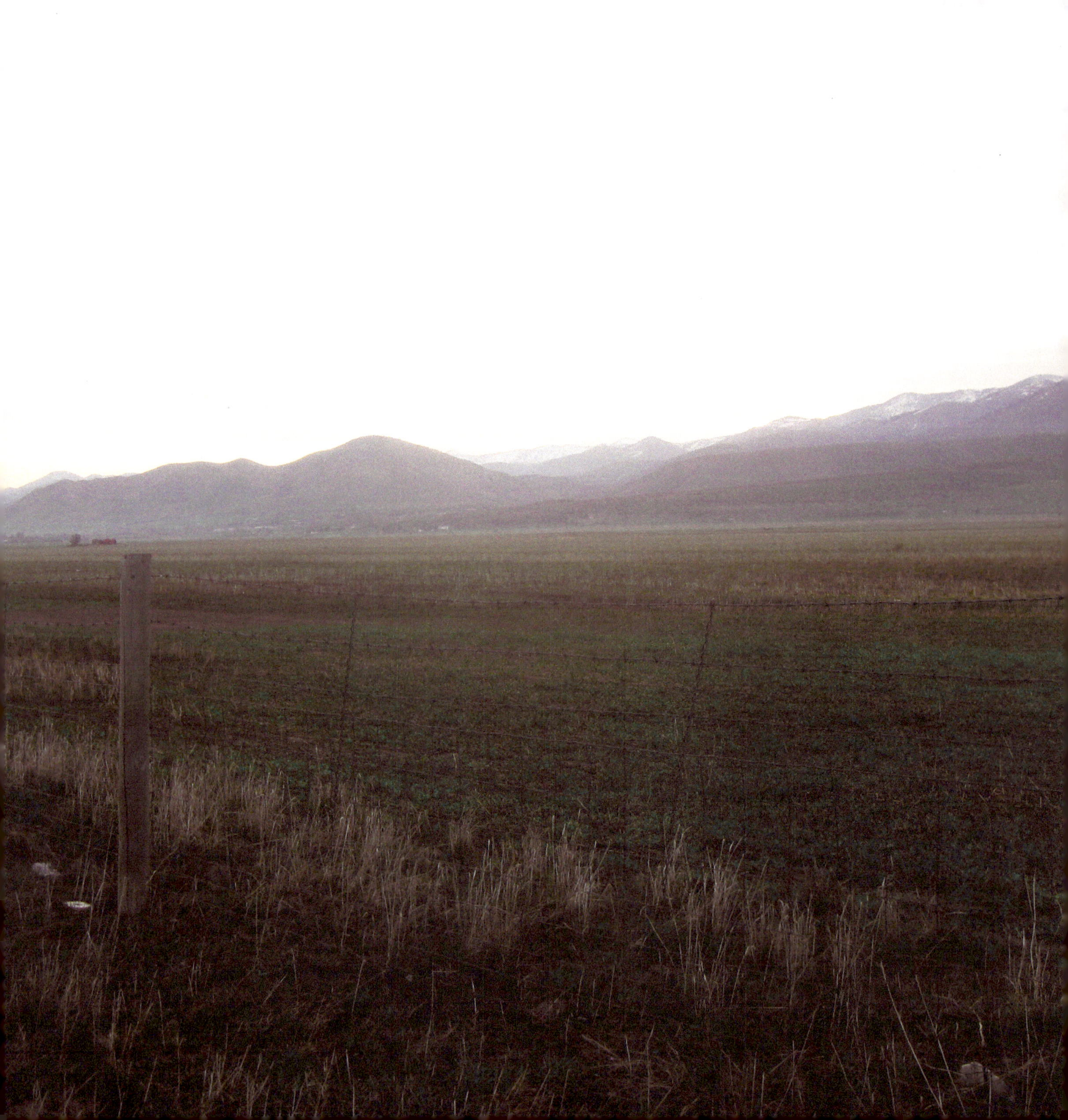

You are stronger than you think!

At times it seems as if the drudgery of life leaves its sting and the bite has not only bruised our broken spirits, but it depletes us of much needed hope and faith. We feel broken down and alone.

When we have lost an individual battle and are wounded on the road to recovery, this is when we need Heaven's help more than ever. We are not alone and yet too often we let loneliness latch onto us and that leaves us feeling rejected. When that happens, we feel abandoned and what's worse, we abandon our sound thinking and begin to believe irrational thoughts about our value. We feel devalued, which determines how we act, what we say, what we do, how we live our lives, the friends with whom we associate, and what we allow to influence us. But these feelings of inadequacy can be overcome when we realize we have priceless value. We have always had it. We were born with it. It does not and cannot decrease with each new disappointment we incur. Our own value increases day by day as we live life. Don't devalue you!

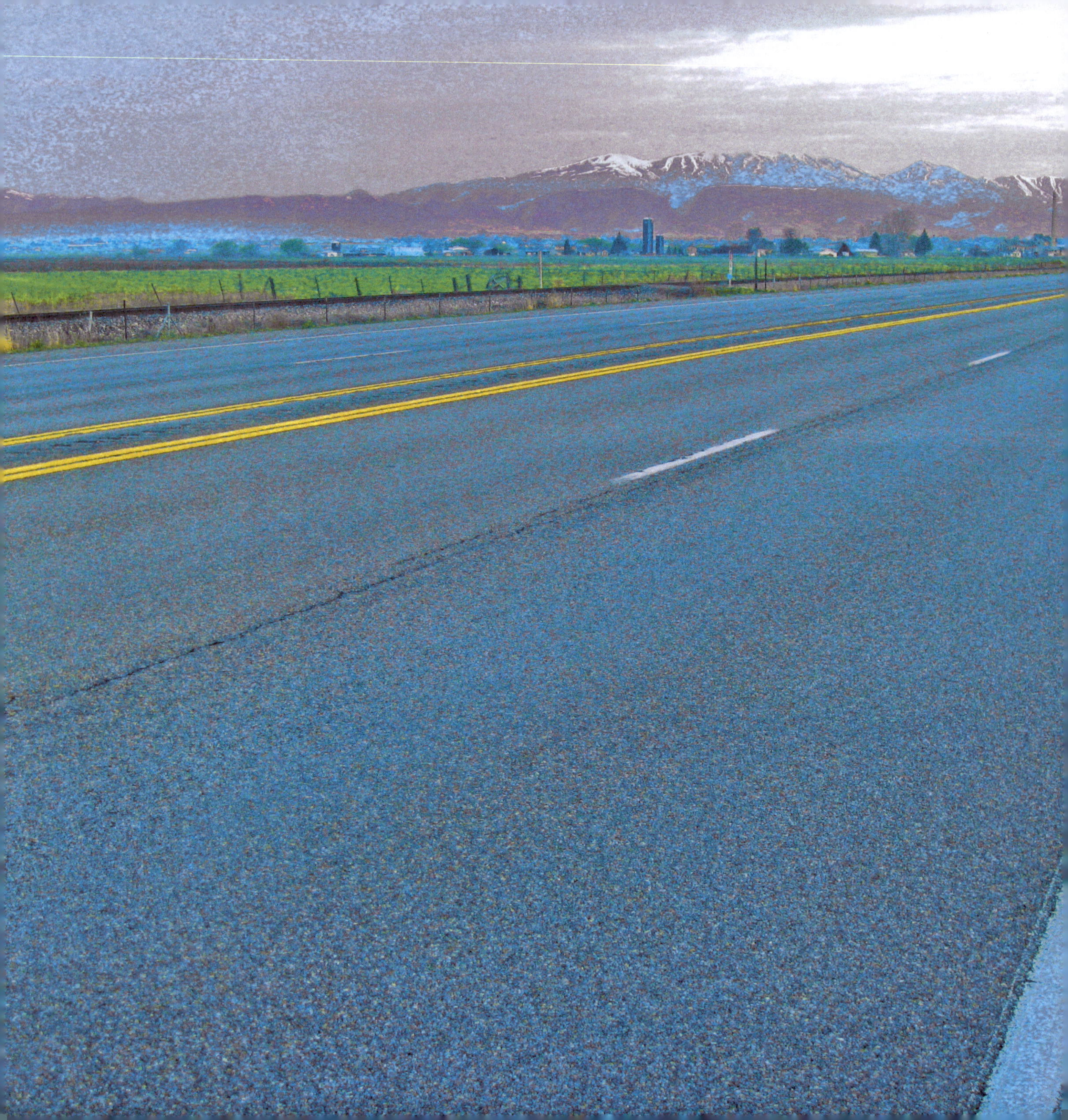

How can you obtain your goals?

On page five we talked about the importance of writing down goals. It is important to set goals, but if you do not define and measure your progress in completing your goals, then you most likely will find it difficult to obtain them. Define, measure, and obtain!

Create ***Micro*** and ***Macro*** Goals

Micro goals are all of the little steps along the way we take to help us accomplish the main goal which is the Macro goal. Any worthwhile goal will take time and effort. It will not be completed quickly or be accomplished with a snap of a finger. This is why it can be difficult to focus on and complete what we set out to do. We often cannot see the end in sight and quickly lose sight of our dreams of accomplishing what we planned on doing from the start. This is where the Micro Goals come in to play. These are smaller and easier to accomplish daily to-dos that help us get closer to the end results we desire. Each step forward is a step in the right direction and we feel a sense of accomplishment every day.

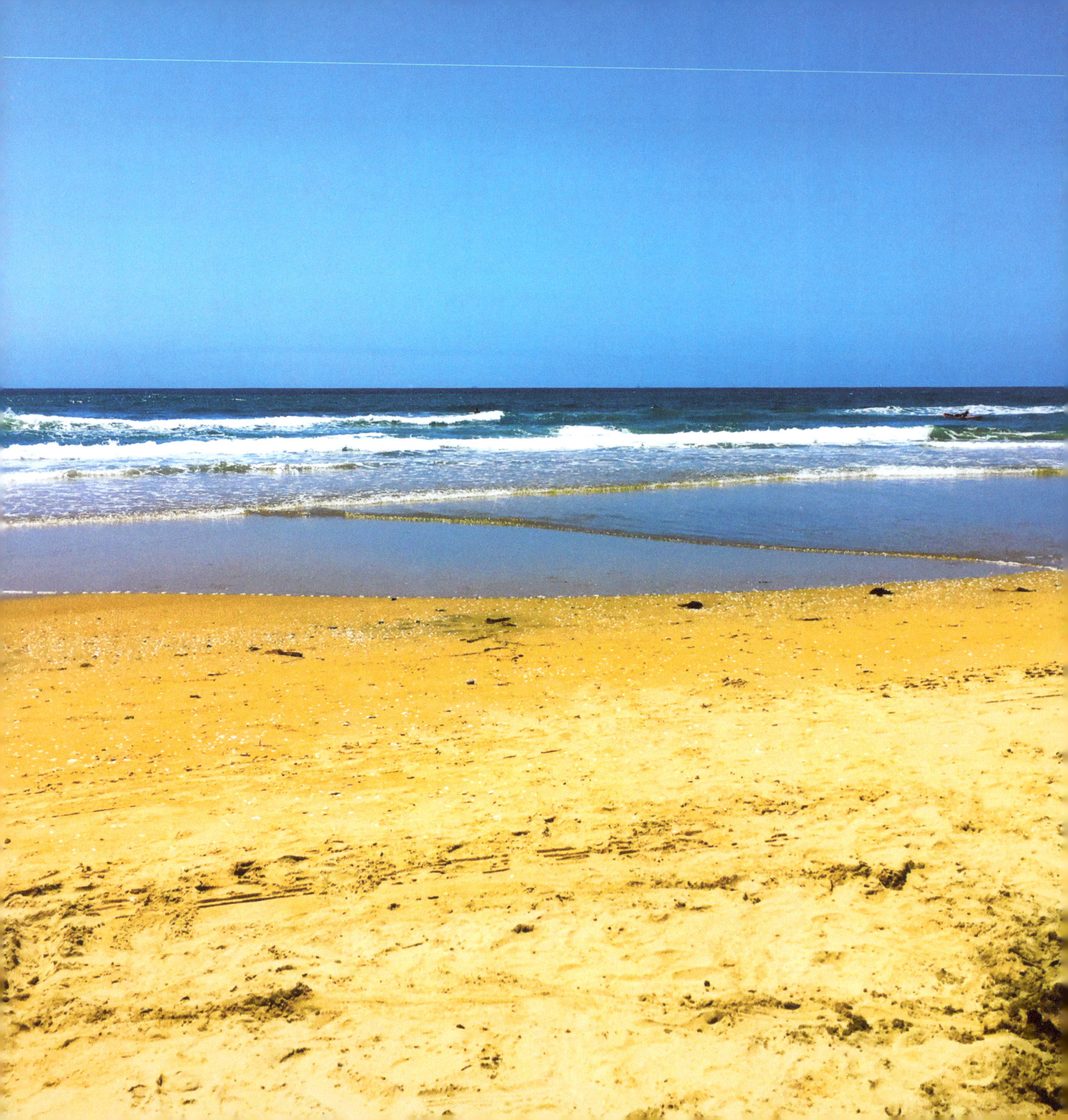

Relax and take it EASY!

Too often, we become wound up like an over-wound clock that ticks to an ever accelerating time. We either want time to speed up or slow down so we can accomplish more and fill up more time. Time, as we know it, continually ticks on and is a slave to no one. We, however, enslave ourselves to each second we have and we also routinely schedule our lives away planning everything to the very last second.

What would our days be like if we intentionally decided to set aside the scheduled planner and cut out the calendars we have become accustomed to cataloging? How would our lives change? What would happen if we stopped our second to second scanning of social media and put away all of our electronic devices that distract and disengage us? How would life change? Every now and then, please STOP! Take it easy and slow down. We can often do more in less time and will get more in return when we give up the many distractions around us.

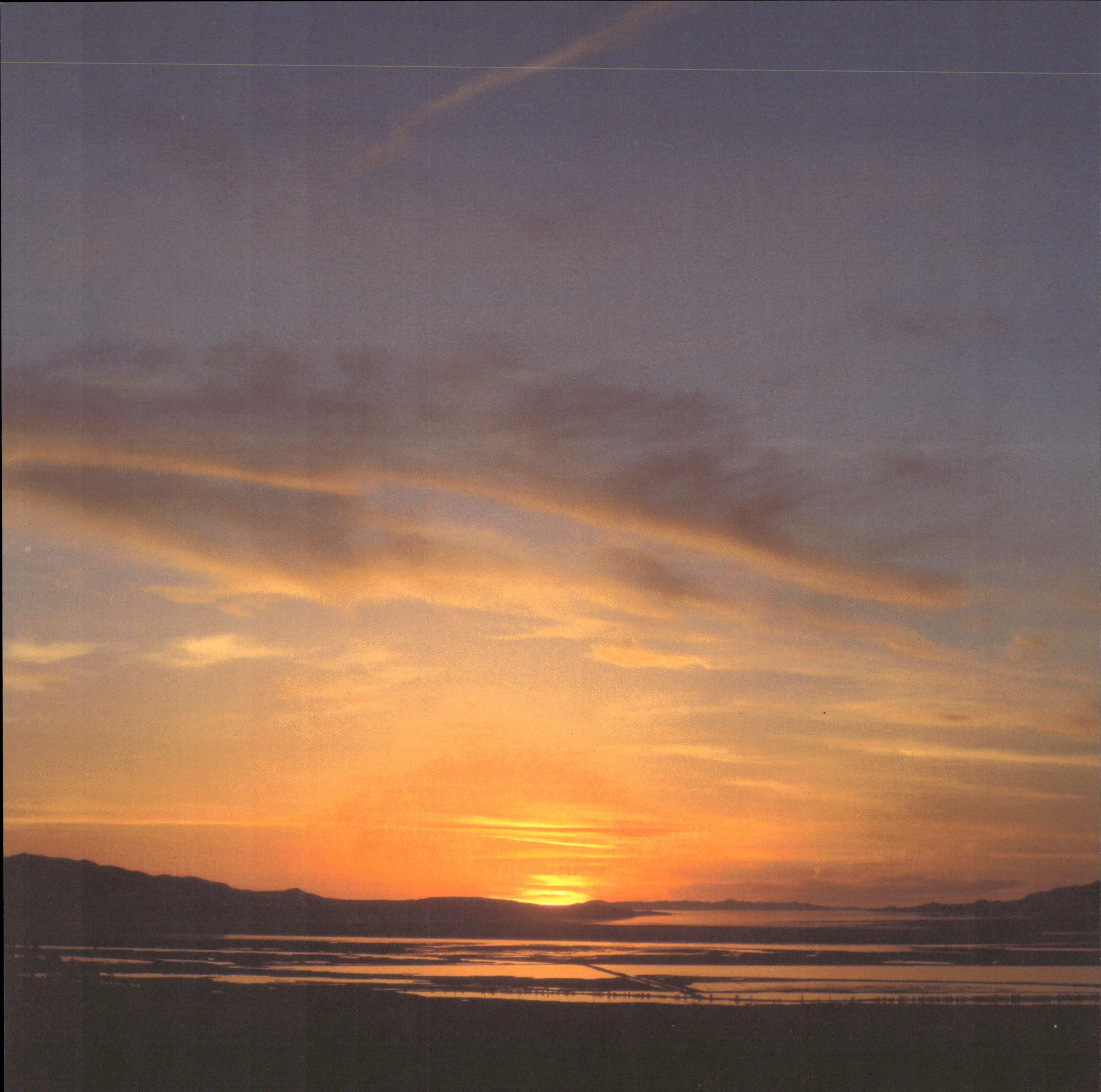

If you believe in yourself, you CAN!

Can and Can't are opposing enemies. On the one hand, if we tell ourselves "We Can" enough times or hear others tell us we can, we develop an attitude or persistent belief in our own ability to accomplish whatever task we are given. This thought enables us to be more effective because we do not put up pretend or imaginary barriers around our beliefs about our abilities, potential, capacity, or the end results. The belief in what we think or know we can or cannot do allows us to persevere and follow through even when plans change, difficulties arise, or we face failure after failure. The mere act of believing in yourself and knowing you can change and improve your circumstances, empowers you to see beyond your present pain and focus on your future in faith. Believing you can accomplish whatever you put your mind to is a start, but having an "I Can" belief is only the first step of faith you will take on your journey toward accomplishment. Once you obtain your "I Can" perspective, then you must actively be true to your convictions. This means going to work! It means being persistent and learning everything there is to learn necessary to accomplish what you want to accomplish. Believe in yourself! You can do it!

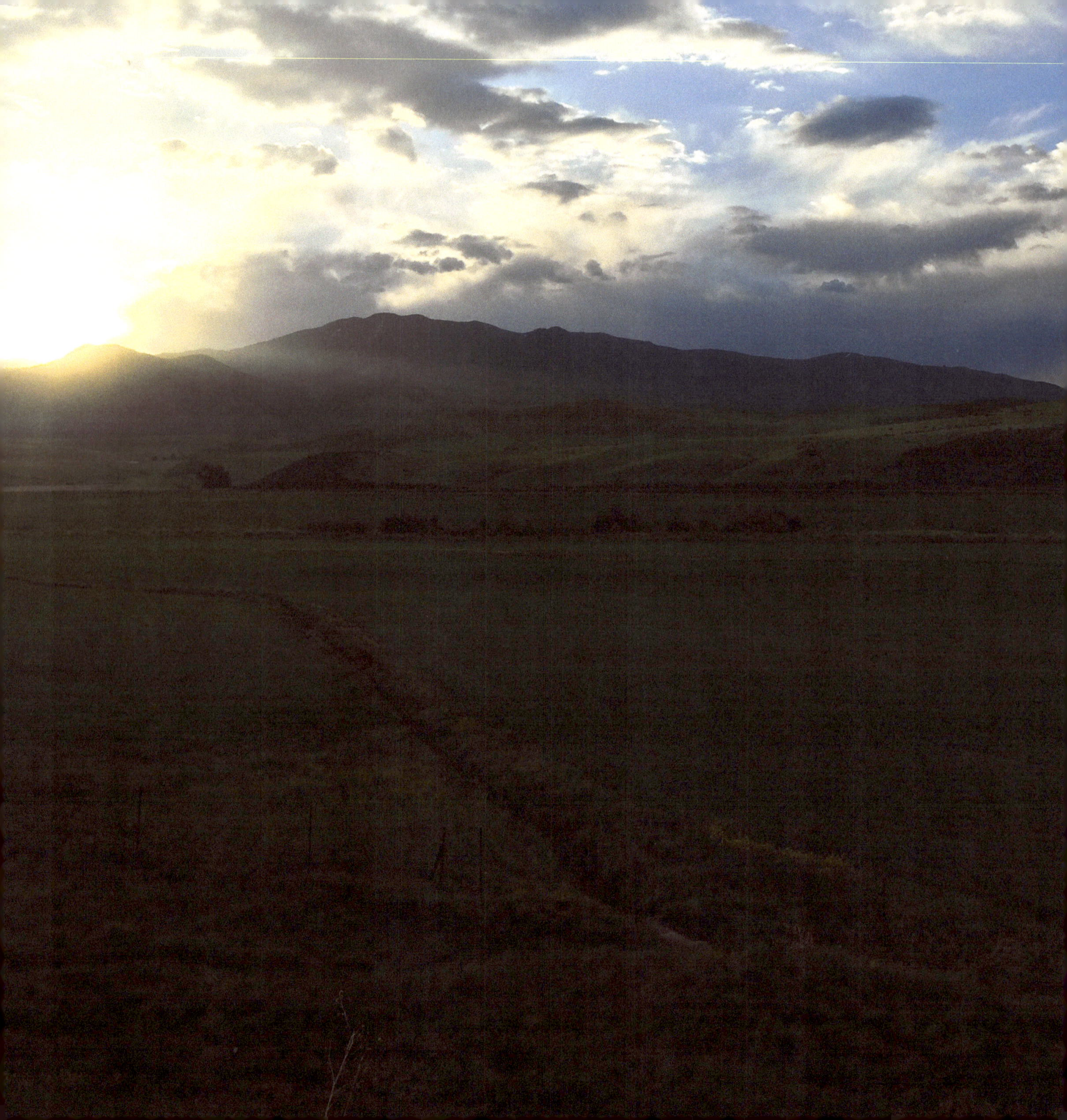

Once you believe, then start to achieve.

Once you obtain an "I Can" belief in yourself and know you are determined to see it through, then you must go to work! Think about that for a moment. You must work as if everything depends on you because you are the one that will make things happen!

Have you ever seen a body builder who lifts weights for a living? Some are shaped and chiseled like statues and others are like solid tanks - immovable and bulging with mounds of biceps. How do they get into shape? How do they stay in shape? What does it take to build that much muscle mass? The answer is everything from diet, to workout regiments, to sleep regulation, to supplements, and in extreme cases, steroids. But the underlying fact is they work out every day. Hours and hours per day are spent doing reps of varied sets of exercises for the upper and lower body.

This same practice is what helps each of us set and achieve goals. We must, at times, repeat over and over again the little daily to-dos that will help us improve. For the most part, it is not some great unbelievable life hack that changes everything. Little things do!

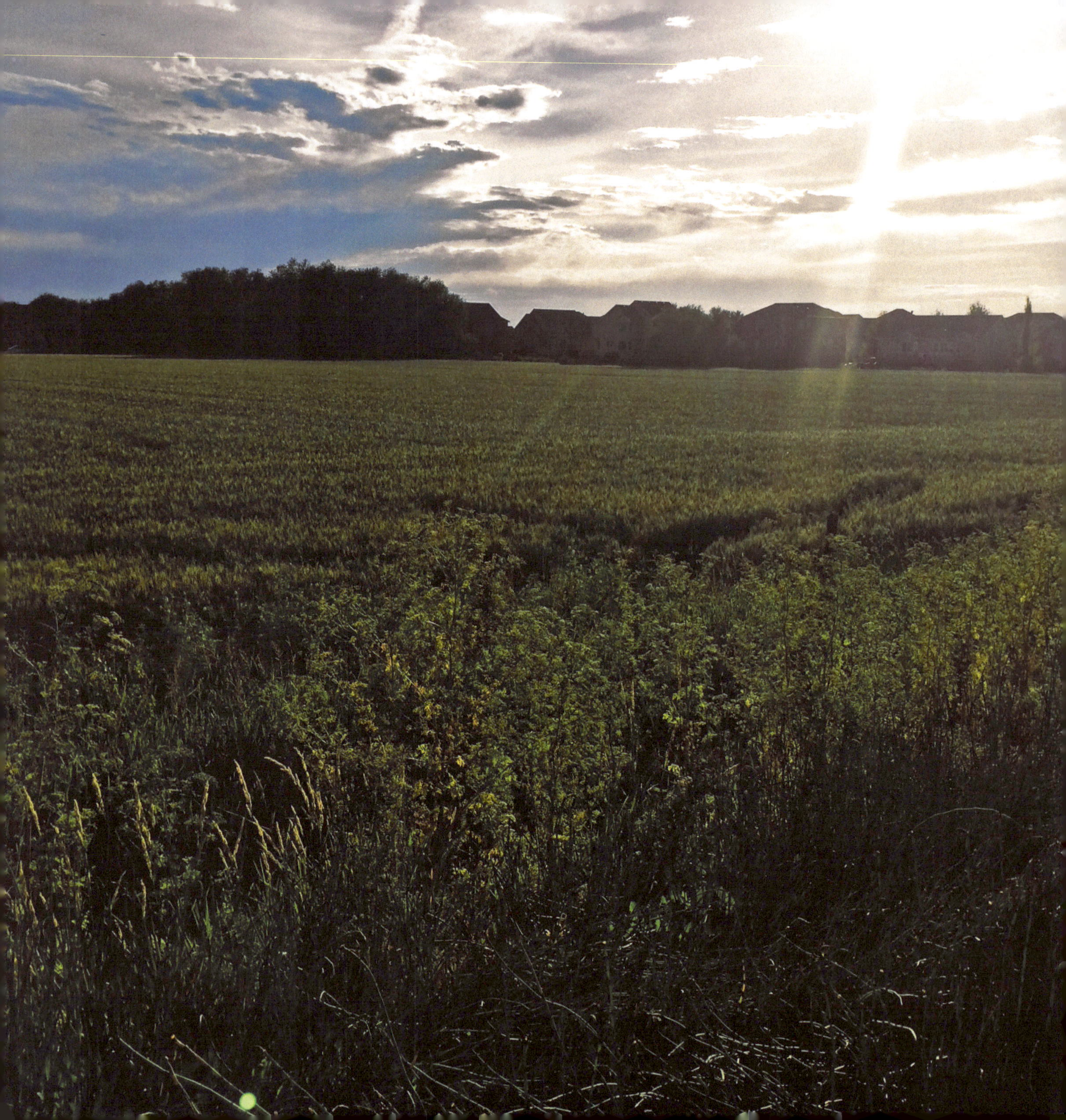

Everyone is IMPORTANT!

When I was in junior high, our school put together some of the students into an organization called the "ESTEEM TEAM." I was privileged to be a part of that organization. We met monthly before school and discussed ways we could help build the other students' self esteem. We decided we wanted to help them realize how great they were. To do this, we came up with various ideas - some of which were motivational thoughts and quotes we would hang on the walls of the junior high. We also created simple and short motivational messages on pieces of paper with candy that we would pass out to students and teachers at lunch and in between classes. This was a simple reminder that *they* were wonderful and we appreciated who they were and all they did each day. We occasionally asked the janitor to open individual lockers so we could decorate them inside and out with balloons, candy, hand-written thank you notes, and little gifts. It was powerful! Start your own esteem team today!

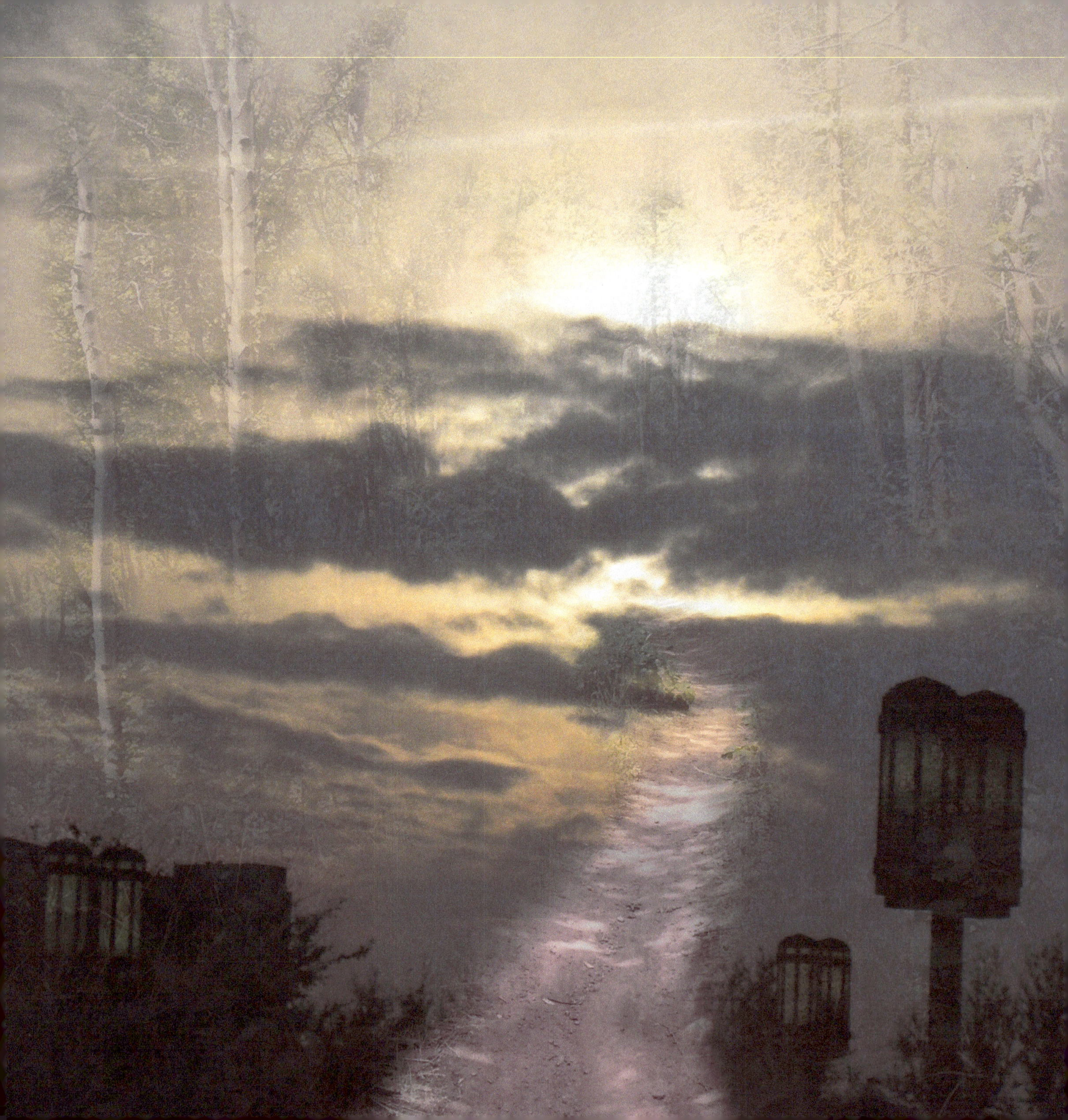

Where are you going in life?

You have the ability to map out and plan the greatest trip you've ever taken. This truly is the trip of a lifetime and only you can take it because it is your destination and personal journey. You can go anywhere and do anything because you are in the driver's seat.

So...

What will you do?
Where will you go?
What will you learn along the way?
What is your primary goal throughout your journey of life?
What will you do when you go down the wrong path?
What will you do when your mode of transportation stops when you get a metaphorical flat tire, or you are in an accident that completely changes your destination?
What are you hoping to experience, learn, and do?
What are you waiting for?

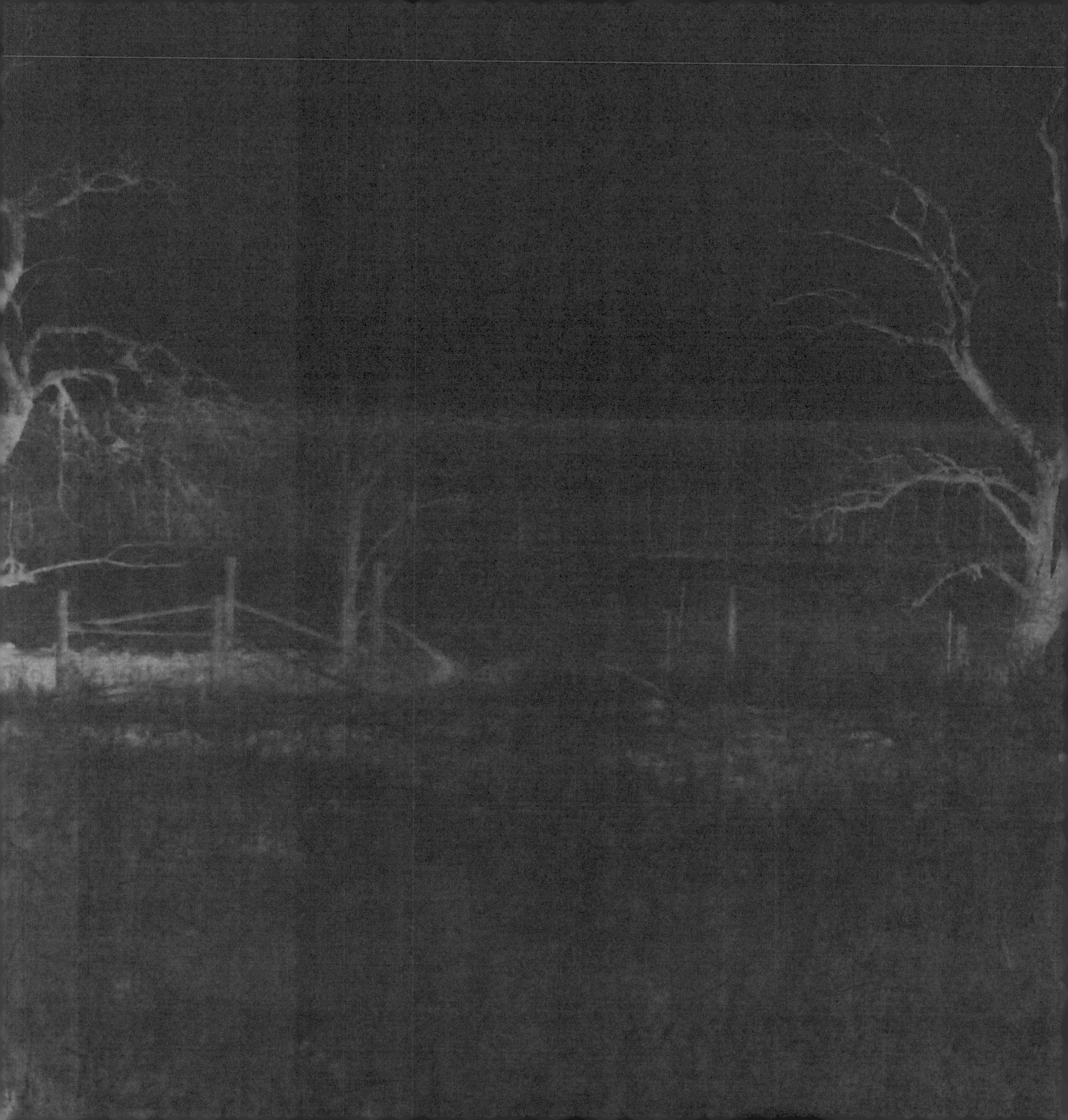

What are your dreams?

Have you ever taken time to write down your dreams? Both the dreams you dream at night and the daydreams you dream during the day? You could think of it like a dream diary where you explain every detail about what you hope for, dream about, envision, plan to do, pray you will be able to do, or expect to do in life. You can also learn a great deal about yourself from writing down the nightmares you have. Don't let your nightmares destroy your dreams.

Darkness can often bring with it an accompanying feeling of unrest, uneasiness, and uncertainty. We cannot see everything clearly. Our vision is limited so our understanding is left to our imagination. We do not see clearly and we fear the worst. When light comes, it illuminates our minds because we see the clear details that had once caused us so much pain and fear.

Wake up and open the shutters to allow the sun to shine through and illuminate your understanding. Things will seem clearer when you write down your thoughts and begin recording detailed ideas to turn you dreams into your reality. Dreams do come true!

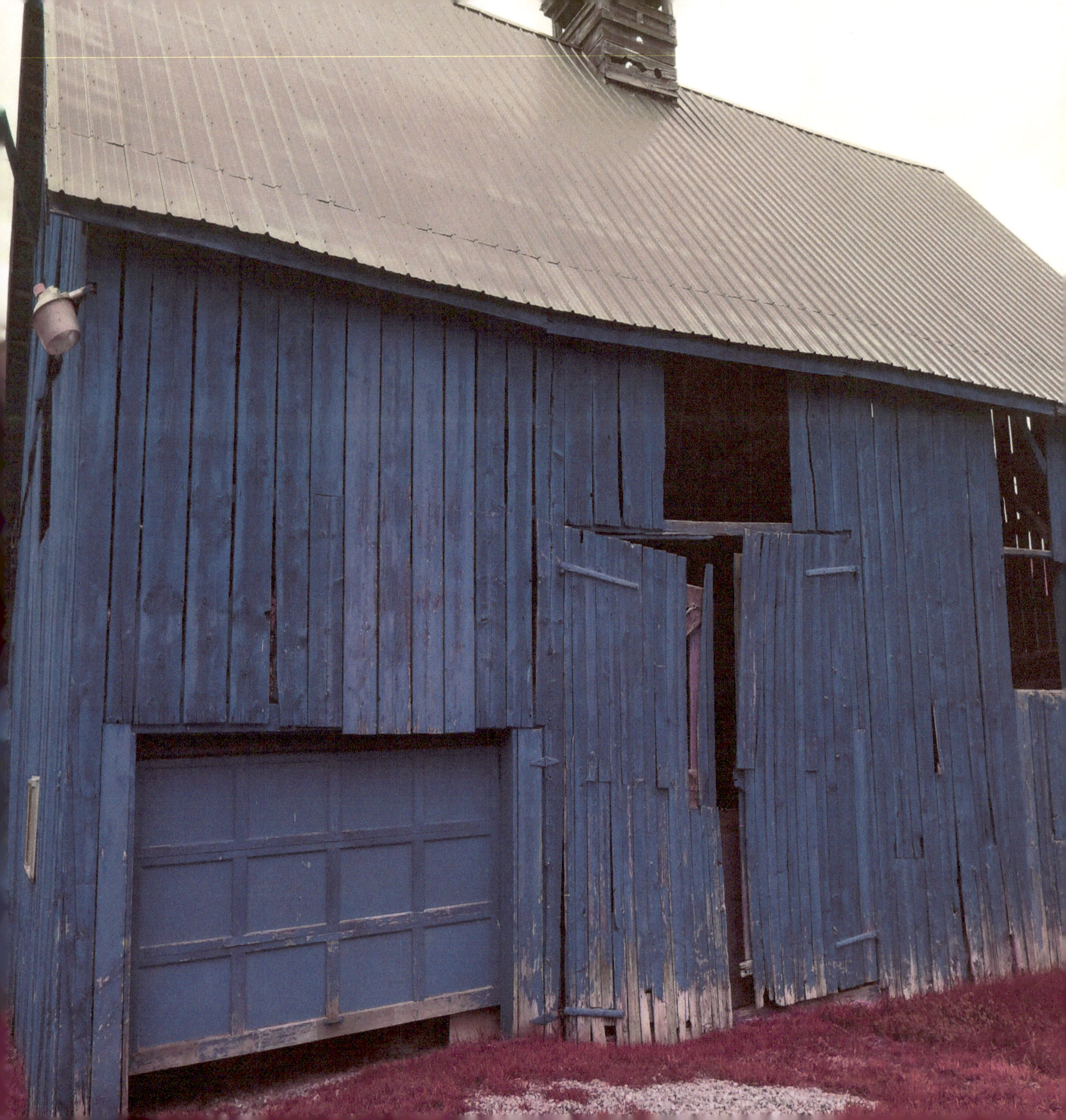

Move forward in faith!

Let's face it, life can be extremely difficult to juggle and at times even the most organized individual feels like they are spinning out of control. There are so many obligations, priorities, tasks, responsibilities, checklists, goals, meetings, commitments, and a never ending list of well meaning "good" activities that all seem very important. We decide between good, better, and best, and ultimately stand behind our decision. When we decide to pursue one activity we must decline other activities no matter how good they are. It's about choosing. We learn to prioritize the best in life.

Sometimes work is extremely rewarding and satisfying because of the problems that are solved, people who are helped, and lives that are changed, saved, and impacted. The list goes on and on. What we dedicate our lives to and where we spend most of our time is meaningful to us and those around us. The problem is when success in one area of our lives comes at the expense of a failure in another area. This often happens largely in two areas - the workplace and the family. We must learn to balance work life and the family life. Both are important, but always put family first!

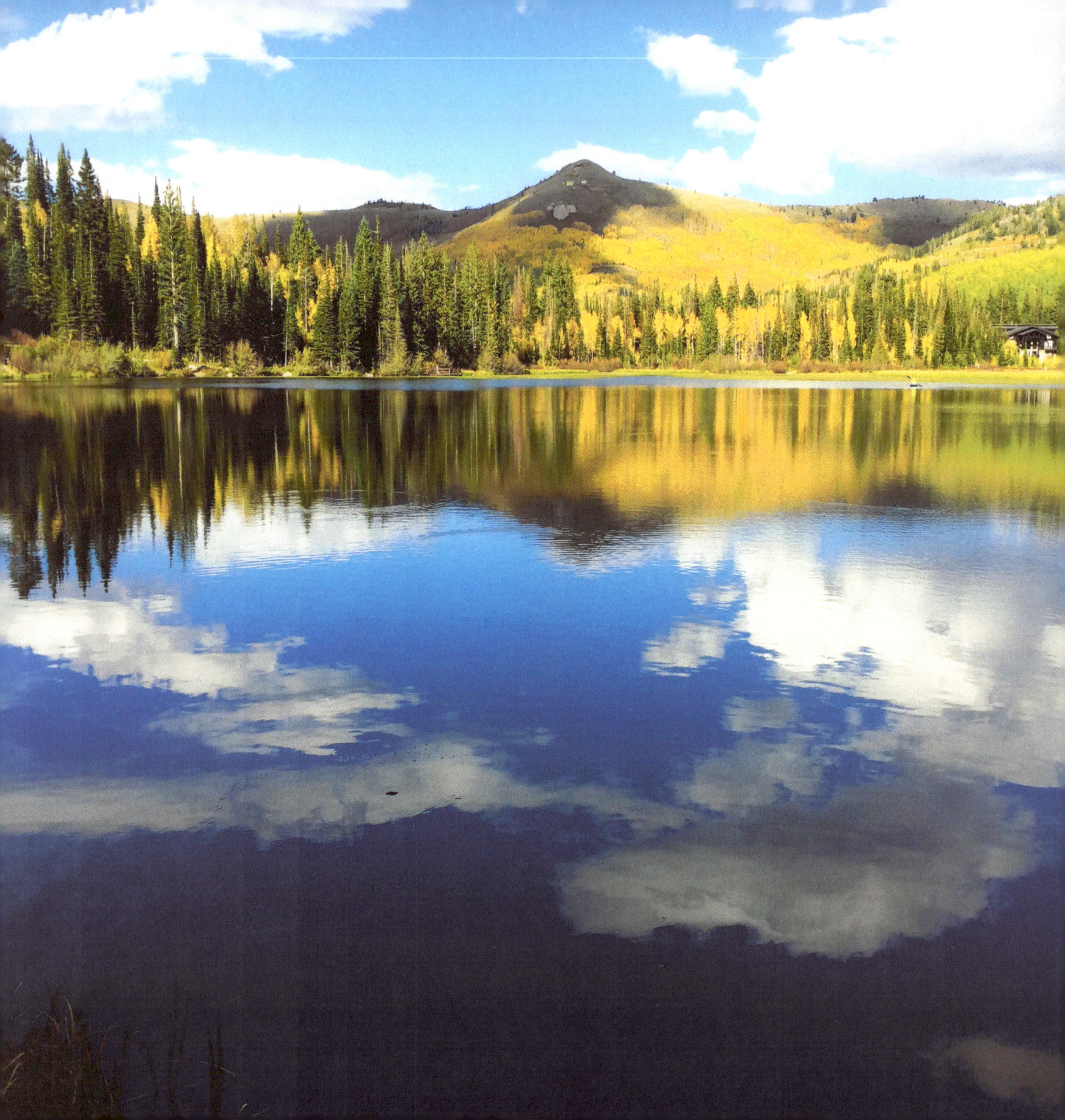

Think Optimistic thoughts!

Do you think your thoughts can help you *and* hurt you? Can your thoughts hurt others as well?

The answer is yes to both questions. Our thoughts can affect us personally. Others can feel the effects of our thoughts because they turn into actions, facial expressions, gestures, verbal and non-verbal reactions to situations, events, and conversations.

What we think about ourselves and others influences the way we behave. This also impacts how we live and who we become.

If you think of yourself as a failure, you will ultimately live up to your own held beliefs and will begin to act in such a way that will perpetuate failure. Thoughts lead to beliefs that can damage your image of yourself and your self-worth. This way of thinking can cause you to mistakenly believe you don't measure up, aren't good enough, pretty enough, educated enough, or capable enough to do anything. That simply is not true. Think positively! Believe in you!

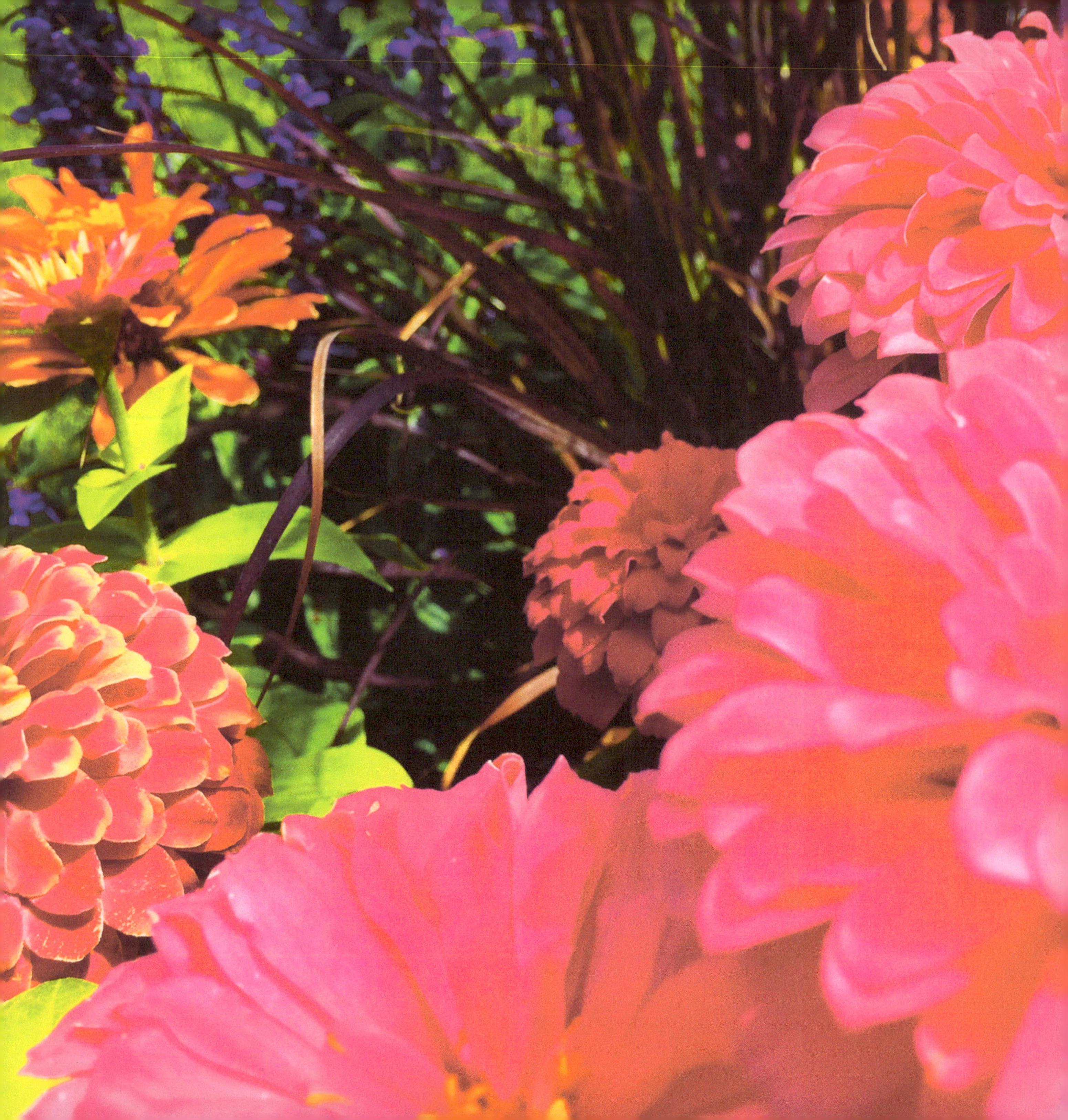

Practice what you preach!

What you say and what you do are very different. Words are often not as meaningful as actions. Most people will say what they hope to accomplish, but are not committed or determined enough to actually do it. We all have been guilty of doing this at one point or another in our lives. But we can stop talking about getting things done and start doing what we have always wanted to do.

Have you ever heard the saying, “Talk is Cheap!”? That means saying we will do something does not help us do it. It is more than talking about setting goals, we must actually do what is necessary to accomplish what we are intent on accomplishing. How do we do that? It is done one step at a time, minute by minute and day by day. We can do a little bit each day, but that little bit adds up to mounds of accomplishment. See something that needs to be done and do it!

BE a POSITIVE influence on others!

One negative thought, gesture, slanderous word, action, unkind behavior, or any other deliberate demonstration of pessimism, unhappiness, frustration, anger, annoyance, unkindness, or unpleasantness has a negative effect and soon everyone becomes disturbed. As smiles wane, the sadness surfaces and the entire community speaks ill of each other, gossips, lies, and can't wait for each day to end. These individuals are filled with darkness and it spreads and entangles others in a formidable web of woes. Watch out for negativity!

Positivity begets positivity. One positive thought, gesture, word of encouragement, kind deed, or caring expression of affirmation can and does change lives. It is a snowball effect when one smile can instantly lead to two smiles and soon those smiles and happy faces compound into an entire community of happy people.

Whatever you do, don't trudge and drudge through darkness when there is so much light around you. **Smile at everyone!** Say positive, kind, and uplifting words of encouragement and **BE HAPPY!**

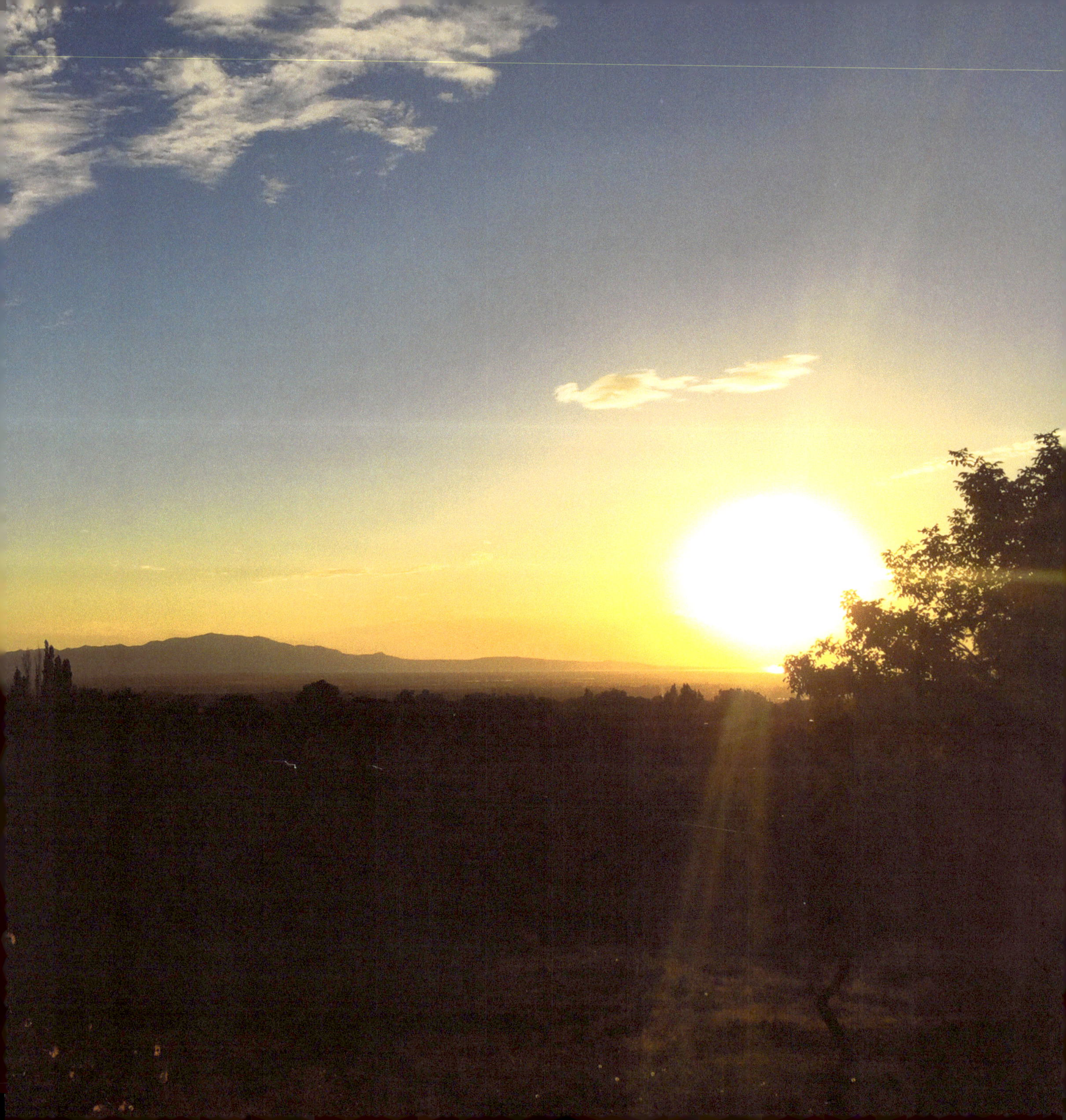

Today is a NEW day!

Whatever struggles you have experienced in your past, let go of them and move on. Whatever heartaches, anger, frustration, and despair you have felt in days gone by, let them be gone. Whatever degree of physical, emotional, mental, spiritual, or any other detrimental feelings of pain you have felt in the past, please learn from them and move forward with faith.

The past is paved with perilous pains that have hurt us, humbled us, taught us, defined us, and prepared us for the present. Today is bright and beautiful with no mistakes. This is your royal road to happiness. It is a journey that begins with one step taken in faith. It does not mean your life is perfect - no one's is. No one has his own perfect path and no one is free from failure, pitfalls, problems, and a life without unhappiness or pain. It does not exist.

With that being said, we have hope and we can watch the sun rise on a new day. Today could and should be our happiest day. We must embark on a journey that is ours and ours alone. No one can walk our life for us, but they can walk with us!

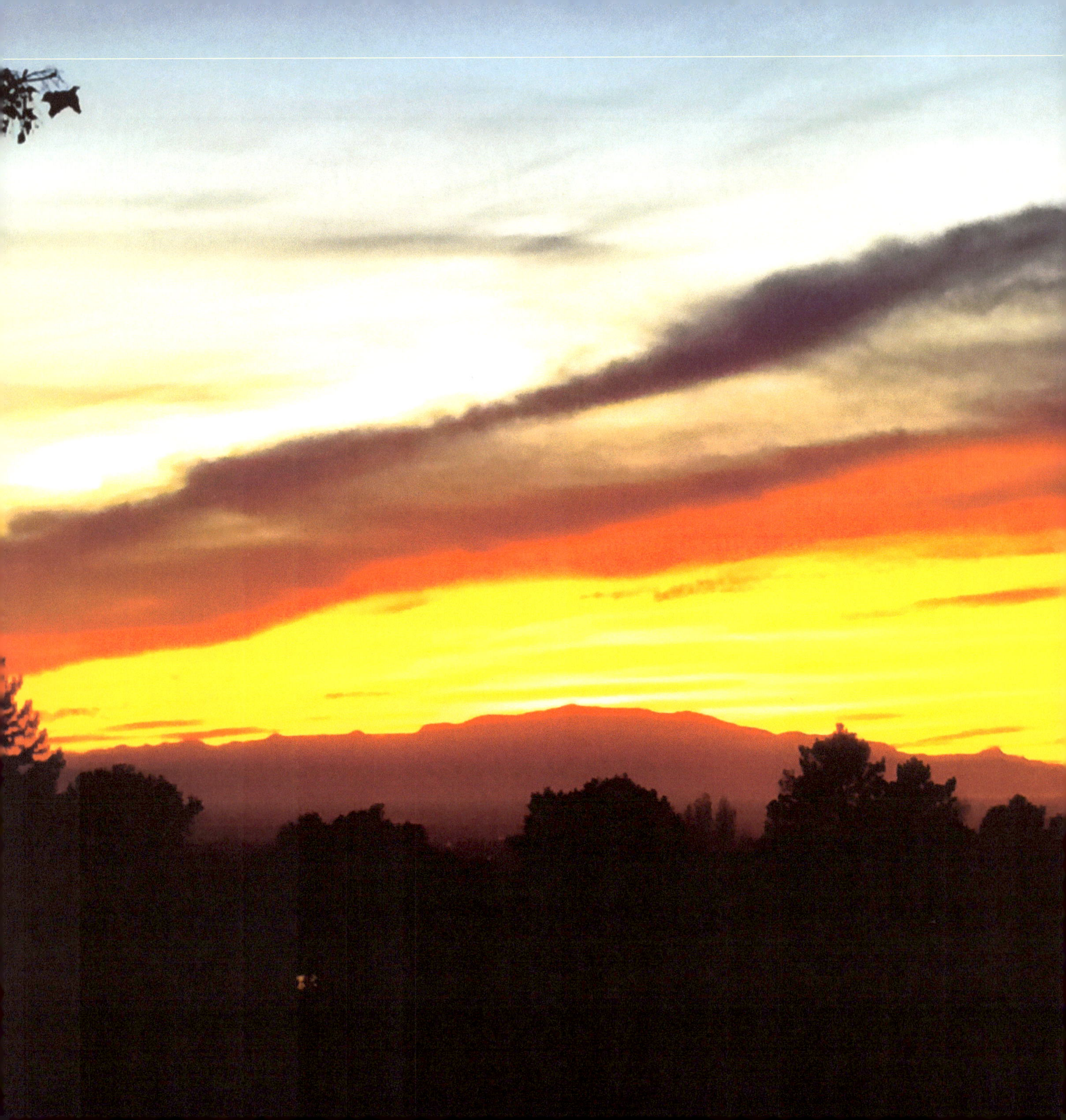

Make the most of YOUR day!

What can you do to make today count? What are you going to do to make today a better day than yesterday was? What can you do to fix or change your perspective, attitude, understanding, speech, actions, emotions, personal ability, and responsibility?

Previously I listed five simple steps anyone can take to make today a little better than yesterday.

Pray - What will you pray for today? For whom will you pray?
Create a daily game plan - What will you accomplish today?
Always be PRESENT - What can you do to eliminate distractions?
Give each day your FULL attention! - What are your main goals or priorities for the day? Are you focusing on deadlines, tasks, items, people, problems, solutions, negativity or positivity? What have you given your full attention to today and why?
Focus on the most urgent/pressing problems and fix those first - This means prioritizing and determining what are truly the most important activities of the day. People always come first. Before deadlines, objects, tasks, quotas, etc.. **People must be your priority!**

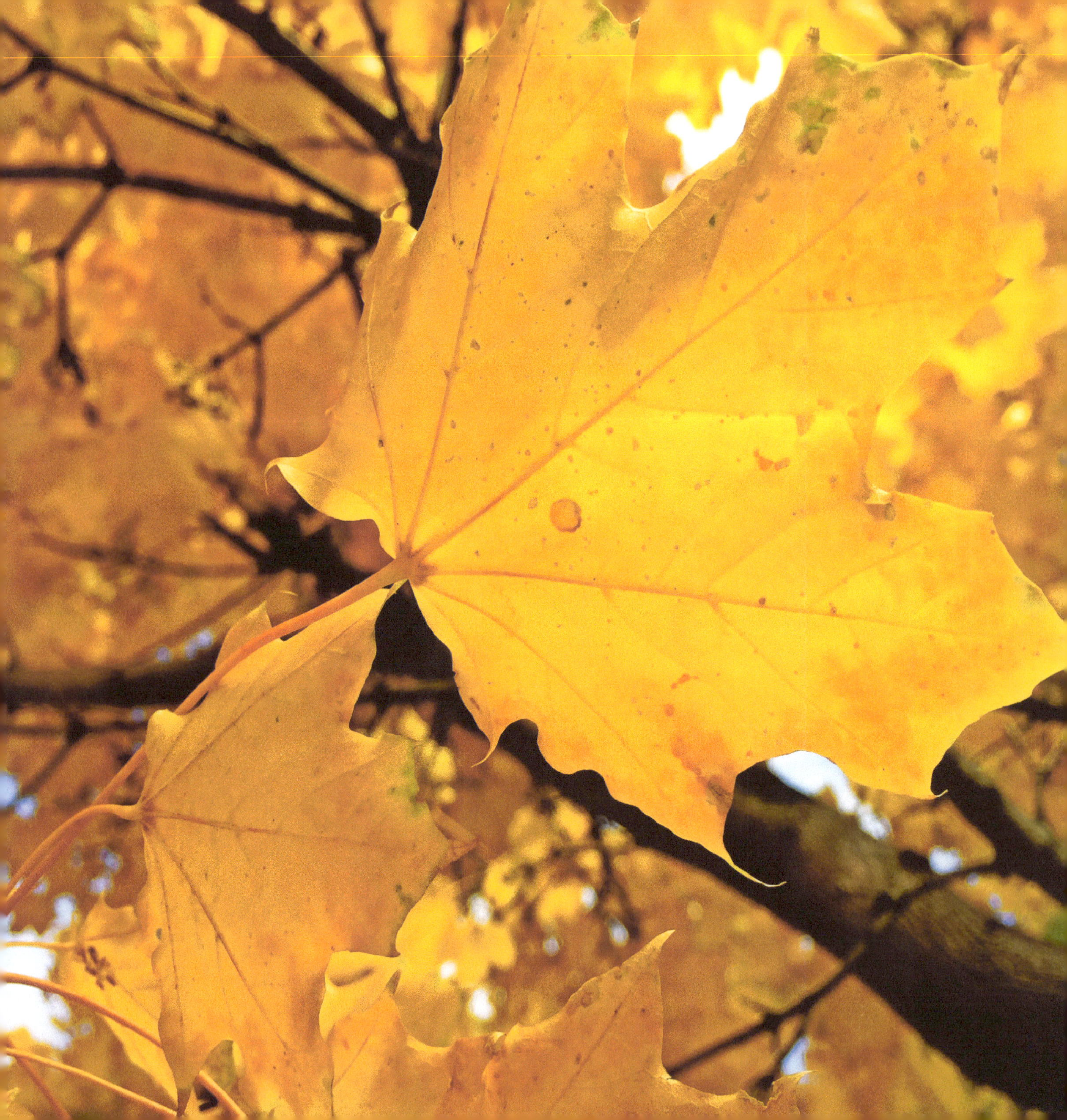

Family = Friends, Faith, and FUN

Do you enjoy your family? It's a simple question and yet the many answers will be varied and diverse. Does your family come first?

Family means something different for everyone. Some people are closer to neighbors and strangers than they are to their families. Others spend so much time with their families that they are almost inseparable. What does it mean to be a family to you? Who is your family? How do you treat your family? What are you doing right now to improve your family relationships? Do you work together as a family? Do you play together as a family? Do you plan family time and vacations you can take as a family?

Our focus should be on the family. As you strengthen your family relationships, you will see that you become friends. Become your own little community of cheering fans that support and strengthen each other. The world is made up of individual families - everyone working together. If you have stronger families you will have a stronger world. Be friends. Have faith and have fun!

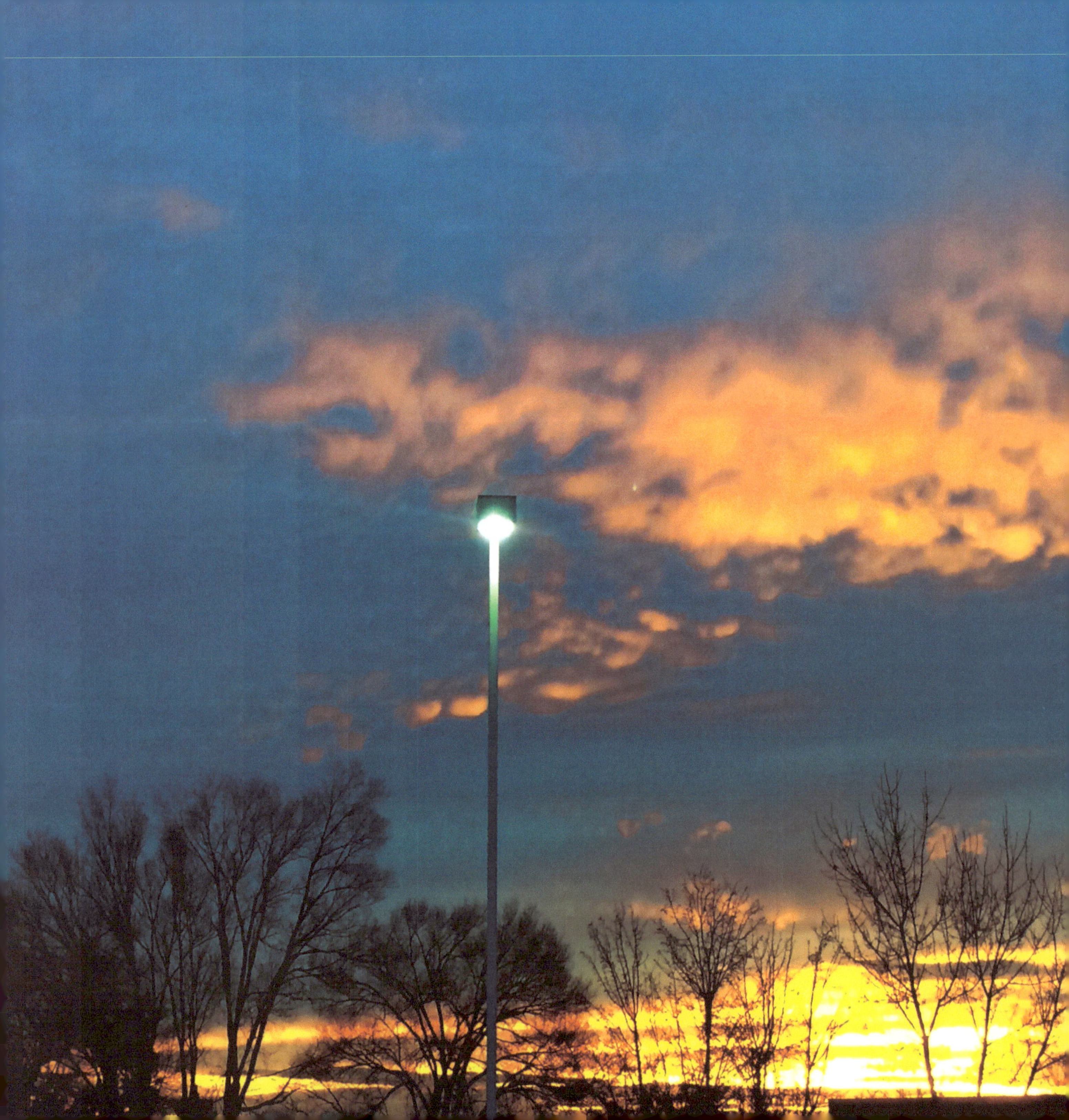

Who are you and who will you become?

You can't see into the future and know what will happen tomorrow or even later today for that matter. But you can plan and prepare to set yourself up for success by having aspirations, setting goals, being ambitious, and knowing what you want out of life.

If you don't decide what you want out of life and don't set goals and prepare for what you hope to accomplish, then you will be tossed about to and fro from one idea to the next. These will be ideas that other people give you unless you take action and make some very important decisions.

Why did you get out of bed this morning?
What do you hope to accomplish today? Tomorrow? Next week? What makes you tick and gets you going? Are you motivated by people, careers, family, fame, fortune, faith? Why are you doing or not doing whatever it is you are doing (or not doing)?

Aspire a little. It's good to reach for the stars and set your sites on higher and loftier goals. Don't listen if people try to put you down.

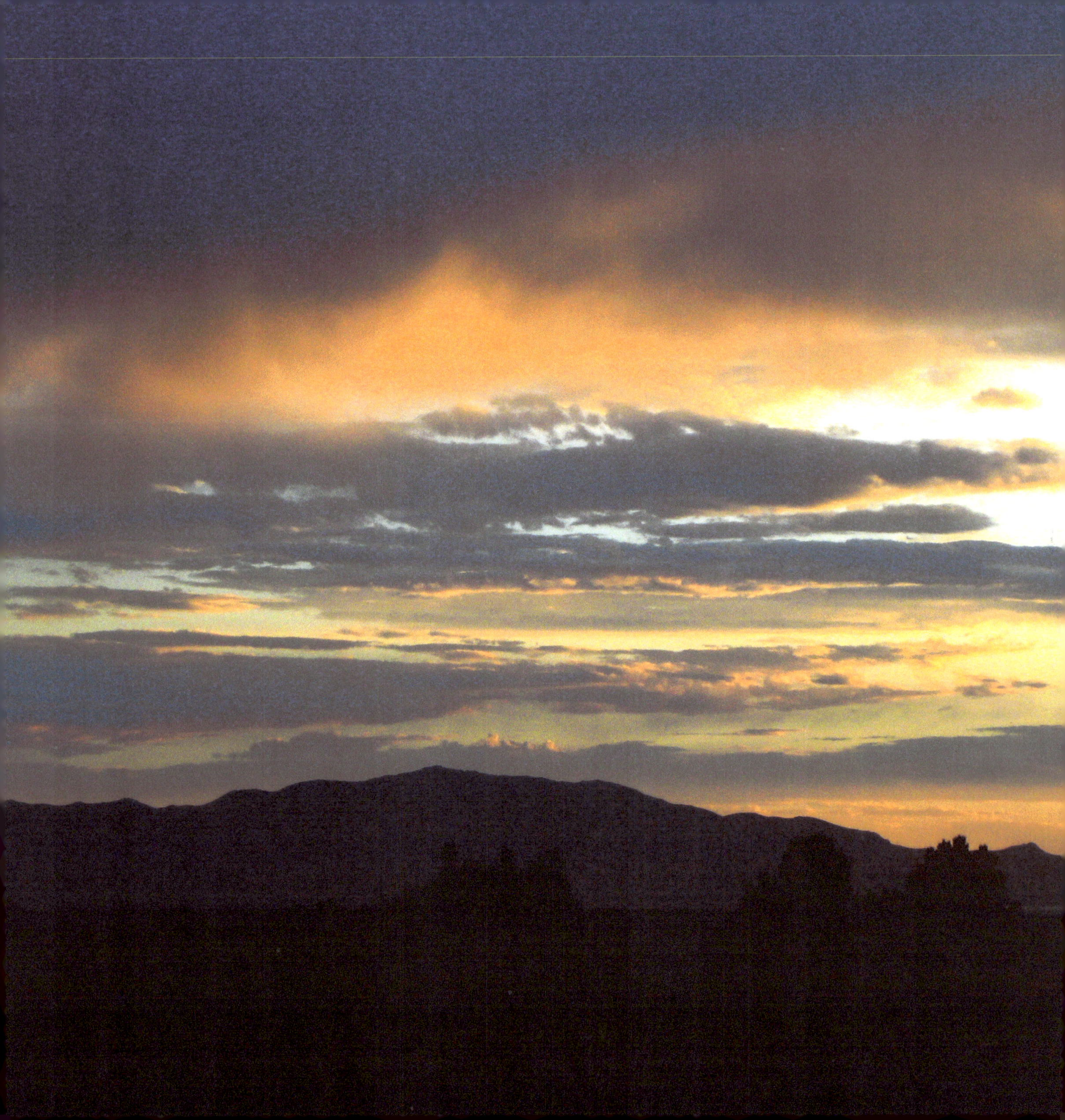

Move forward, onward, and upward.

It is difficult to keep moving forward when everything and everyone is pushing you back. That is how most days feel and it is often how most days turn out. The trees that grow the strongest are the ones that have the most wind blowing against them. They are fighting every minute to stand up against the wind that is trying to blow them down. There are some trees that snap under the pressure and break, but it is often because they do not have the support to strengthen them when they are young.

In this regard, people are the same as plants in how our roots can strengthen us against the influences that surround us. When we are rooted in positivity and optimistically strive to do our best, we have more endurance and willpower to stand up whenever we fall. The wind may knock us down a few times but we are stronger.

It is always easier to digress and take the easy way out when life becomes difficult. But to progress toward greatness, we must fight!

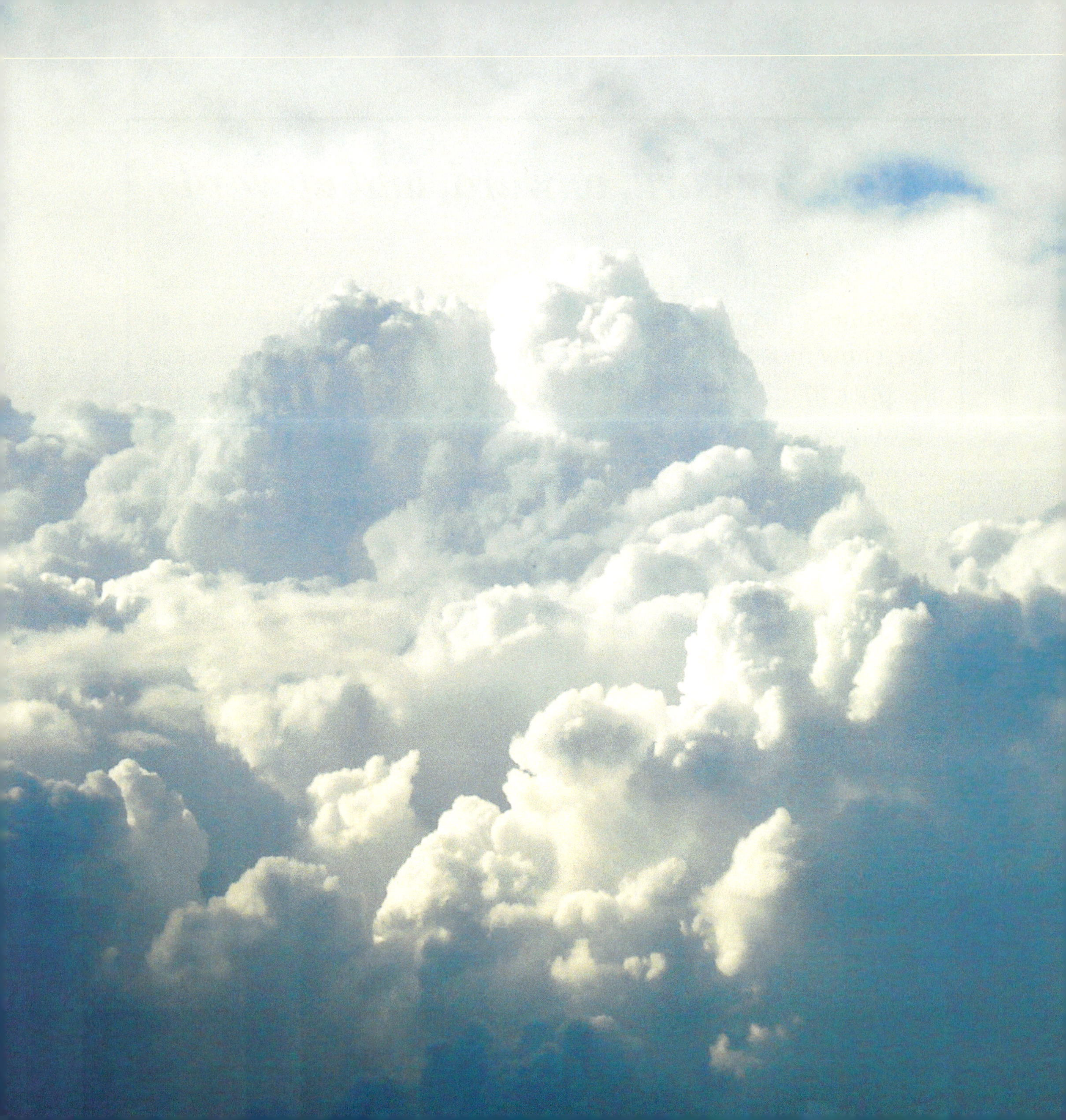

Be patient but persistent!

I remember fishing as a boy with my grandfathers. They were fantastic fishermen and taught us all to fish. But what we really learned was how to be patient.

I soon learned how much patience and persistence is required for fishing. At times we would find a new fishing spot or try new bait, hooks, or rods. With our new approach we started again. We were being taught to be patient and not to give up and quit just because the fish were not biting. Sometimes we needed to change our approach.

So, if at first you don't succeed...Try, try, again - and then repeat, recycle, redo, re-plan, recommit, re-examine, re-evaluate, rework, rethink, retrain, and repair what you have done and don't be afraid to do the same thing tens of thousands of times over and over again. Repetition, when done correctly, is the recipe for success.

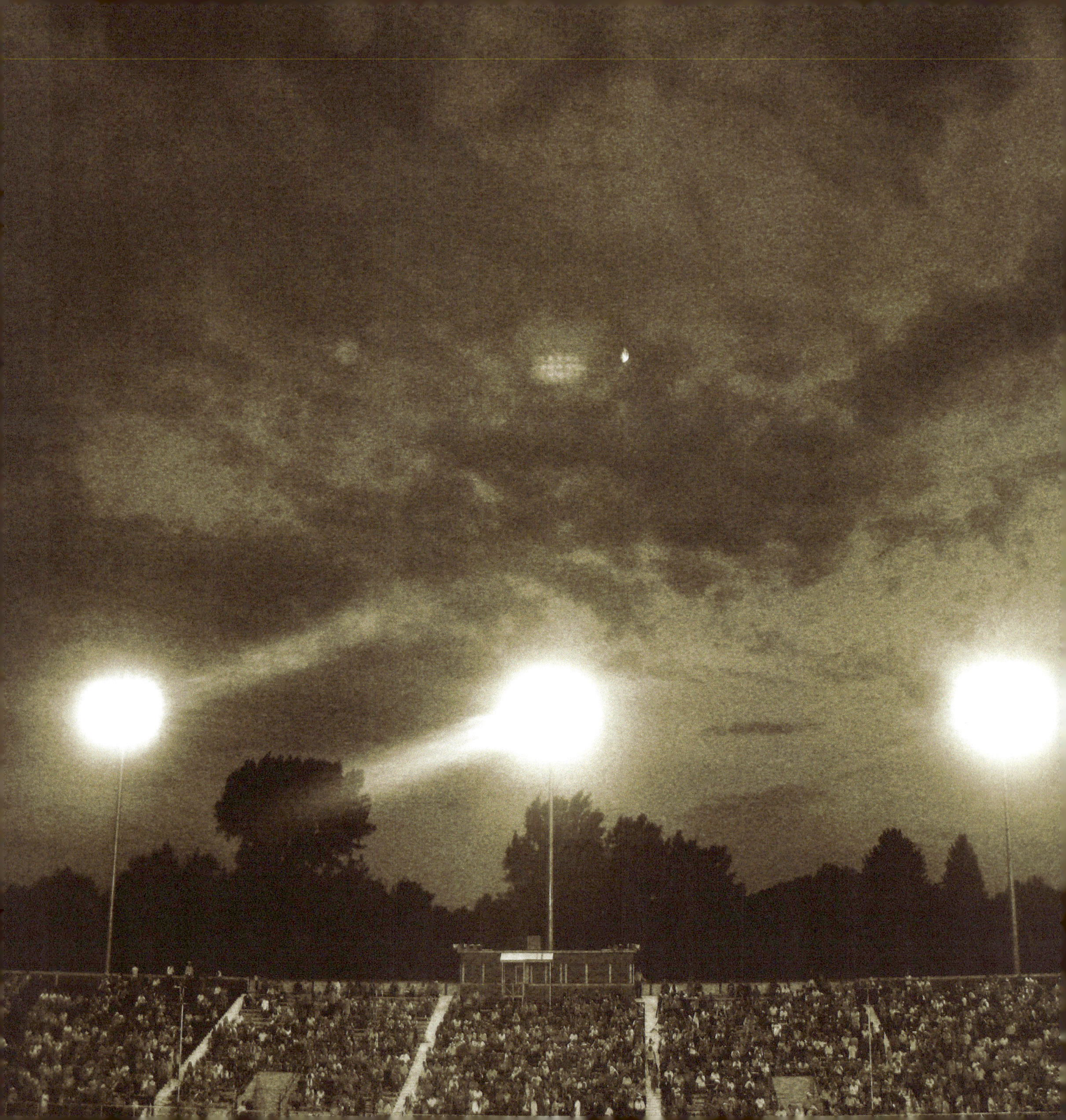

Set and achieve GOALS

Sometimes I feel like goals have become overused, undervalued, unappreciated, feared, and forsaken. Most goals are made at the start of the new year and promptly abandoned after a week or two.

What happens? Why do so many people start or set goals but don't ever do anything to finish or accomplish goals. What changes?

Think of a football team going for the goal! They have a clearly defined goal in mind to move from one side of the field to the other in an effort to score on the opposing team. The other team, however, has that exact same goal. Both sides are fighting to win and move forward while trying to push the other team back. The sides are lined up against each other. Right against wrong, good against evil, one goal working against another. Both teams are doing their best. One team wins.

In life you can set your own goals but you must work on them even when an opposing team is fighting against you. Go for the goal!

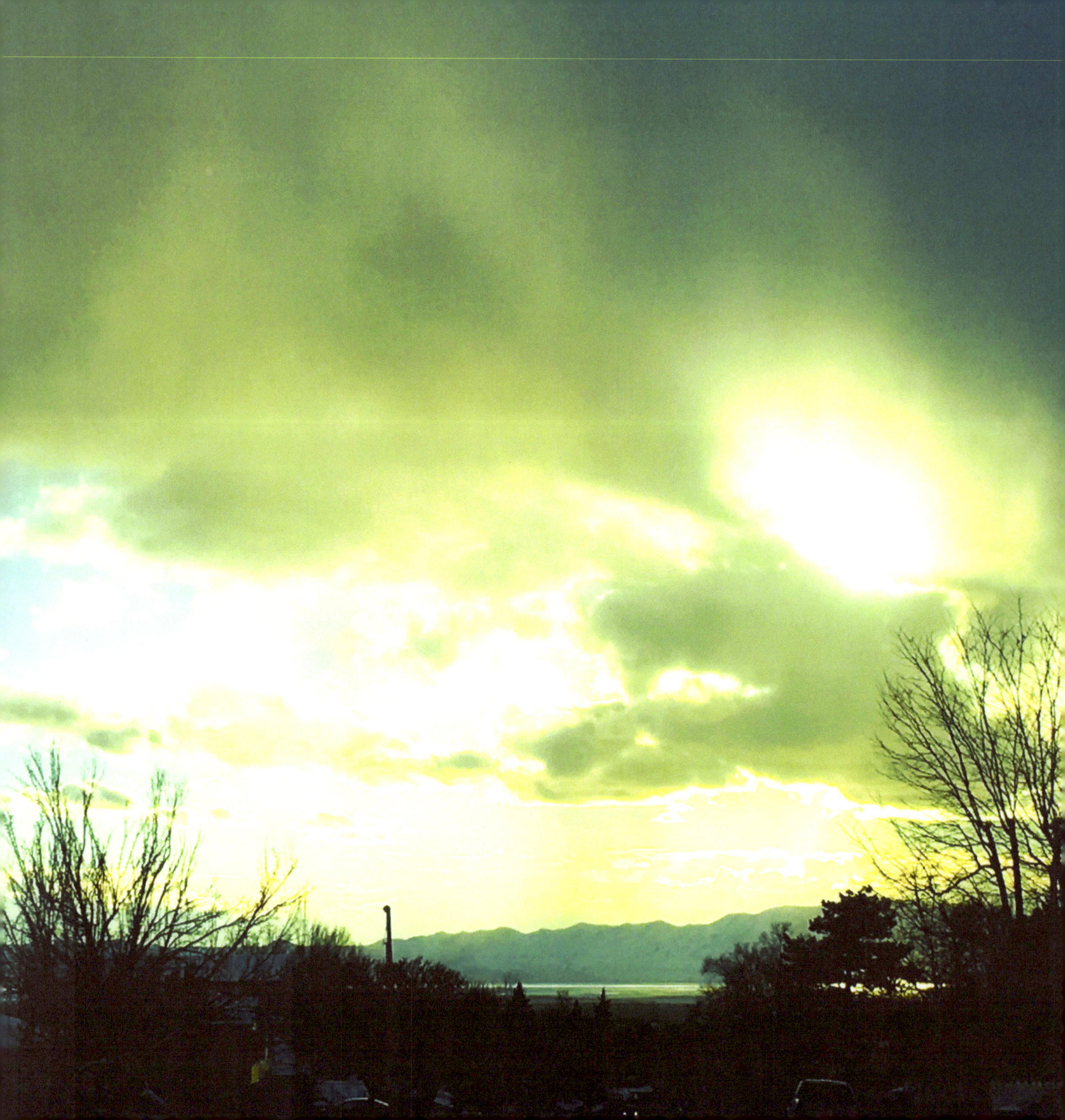

Opportunities are often disguised!

What one person sees as a dire opposition, another may view as a challenge or opportunity. One individual may see setbacks and struggles and another man or woman with similar circumstances will see hope and possibilities. Do you see?

Life is about how we view it and what perceptions we have that can help us or hurt us. Failures are nothing more than stepping stones that can take us in the right direction and help us re-focus our thoughts and intents on our life's mission. Failures actually help us.

Do the following:

Write down a truth about yourself - good or bad. Can you change? Write down a fear you would like to overcome. What can you do? Write down a failure you have experienced and how you can take that failure and turn it into a success story. How can you improve? What can you do to see the potential and possibility of your own abilities even when you only see mistakes, weaknesses, and fear? How can you turn your weaknesses into strengths?

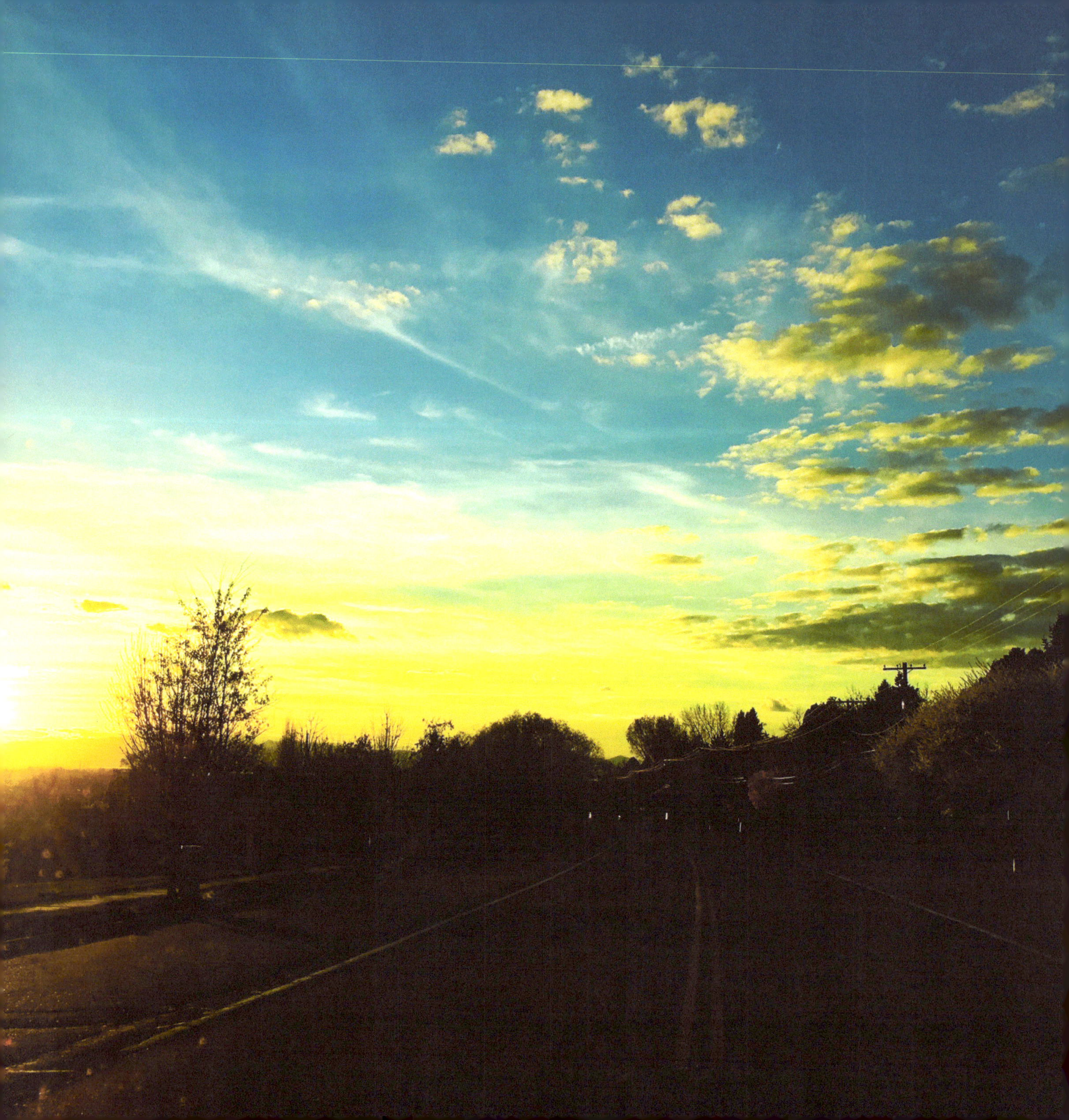

Believe in yourself. YOU CAN DO IT!

The words I can and the words I can't can make or break you. As important as it is to have others believe in you and cheer you on through life, it is much more important for you to believe in yourself! You must believe in your potential and ability! Do you?

It does not matter what others tell you to motivate or inspire you if you do not believe what they say. Their words can be helpful as they push you and move you along. But if you do not believe in yourself, it does not matter what anyone else says in your behalf. You will not believe them so it will most likely annoy you more than motivate you. With that being said, their motivation and belief in you, even if you do not believe in yourself, will help you know you can rely on them and their strength. You can trust their belief in you even if you do not yet believe in yourself. Know that your voice is paramount because what you tell yourself about yourself is more influential than anything anyone else can say about you. Believe you can do anything you put your mind to because you can!

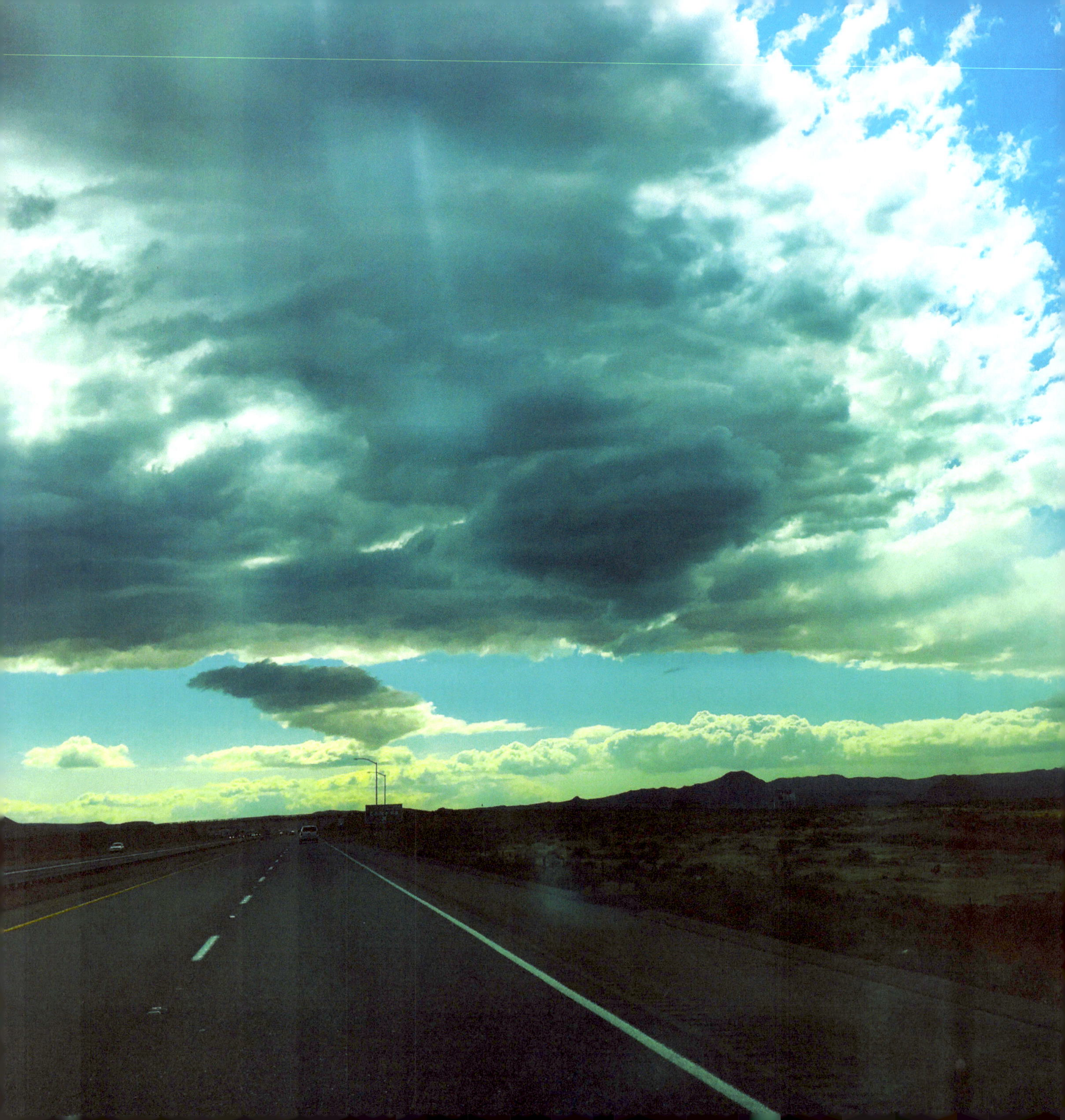

Your future awaits you!

Where will your adventures take you today? Every step you have taken in your life has led you to where you are at this moment. You have an opportunity to move forward and advance and improve and grow. Everything you are learning and every good and bad experience you have had in life thus far has helped you arrive at your present location. But where do you want to go from here? That is the question that each of us needs to ask ourselves every day. So ask yourself…Where will my adventures take me today?

Embrace today. Experience today. Soak it up. Live today as if it will never return because it won't. You have but one day to live today's day. Once the sun sets you can never retrieve today. It will be in the past and will be a memory – something you look back on fondly or try to forget. That is why today is so important. Enjoy it while you have it. Don't let it slip away or go unnoticed. Live today and be present today. Make the most of today! Have a wonderful day today and be prepared for where it takes you. Enjoy each step along the way.

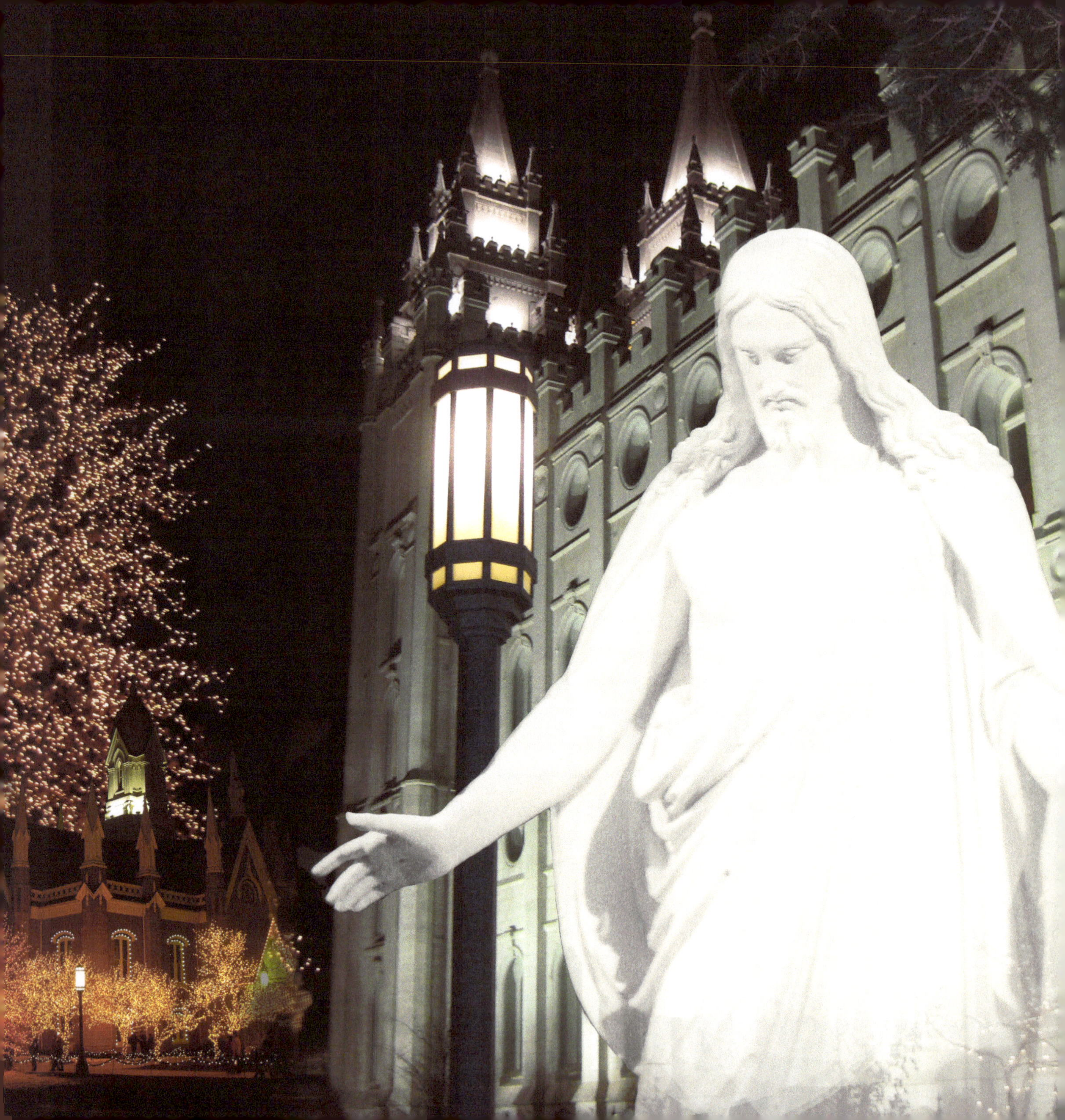

Open your arms to those who need you!

At Christmastime, more than any other time of the year, our hearts are often turned to helping others. We often hum and smile our way through December and hope to bring peace and goodwill to everyone we meet.

Sometimes this happy cloud-like sensation is struck down on the last day of the month. When this happens most people fold up their fun and some tend to stop thinking about others.

Have an open heart and an outstretched hand to everyone who needs you and your help and service throughout the year. Let every day be Christmas as you think of others. Think how you can spread hope, happiness, and a little bit of Heaven each day. The sweet and happy feelings we experience at Christmastime when we are surrounded by family and friends, lit up by the light of sparkling Christmas lights and our favorite Christmas songs, can and should remain with us all year long.

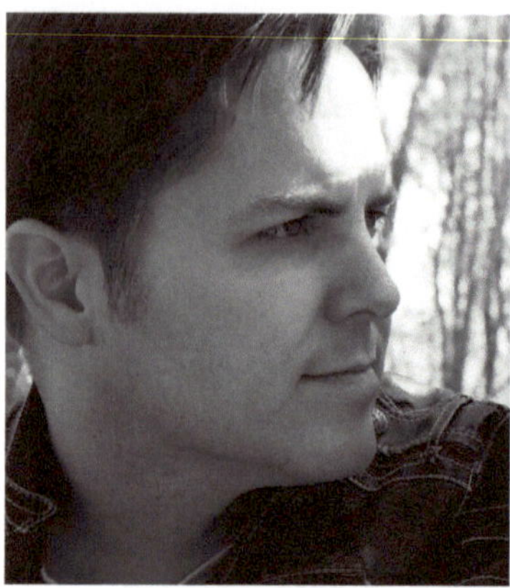

About the Author (Poet)

JERALD SIMON

Connect with me on Social Media

http://musicmotivation.com
http://youtube.com/jeraldsimon
http://facebook.com/jeraldsimon
http://linkedin.com/in/jeraldsimon
http://twitter.com/jeraldsimon

"My purpose and mission in life is to motivate myself and others through my music and writing, to help others find their purpose and mission in life, and to teach values that encourage everyone everywhere to do and be their best." - JERALD SIMON

First and foremost, Jerald is a husband to his beautiful wife, Zanny, and a father to his wonderful children. Jerald Simon is the founder and president of Music Motivation®. He is a composer, author, poet, and Music Mentor/piano teacher (primarily focusing his piano teaching on music theory, improvisation, composition, and arranging). Jerald loves music, teaching, speaking, performing, playing sports, exercising, reading, writing poetry and self help books, gardening, and spending time with his wife, Zanny, and their children.

Jerald created **musicmotivation.com** as a resource for piano teachers, piano students, and parents of piano students. In 2014 he began creating his weekly "Cool Songs" to help teach music theory - the FUN way by putting FUN back into theory FUNdamentals. He is the author/poet of "The As If Principle" (motivational poetry), and the book "Perceptions, Parables, and Pointers." He is also the author of 21 music books from the Music Motivation® Series. He has also recorded and produced several albums and singles of original music.

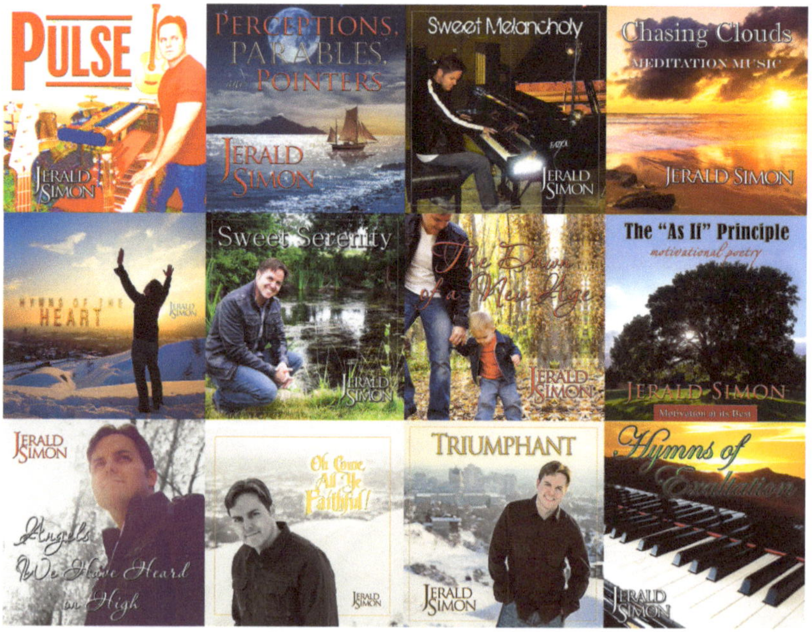

I have several CDs of original music I have composed that I would love to have you listen to. You can listen to my music on Spotify, Pandora, etc., or purchase my music on i Tunes, Amazon, and all on-line music stores. I compose several different styles from hymn arrangements to meditation music, new age piano solos to pop, techno-pop, rock, and even scary Halloween music. Let me know what you think of my music!

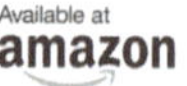

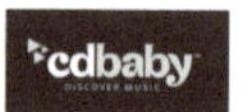

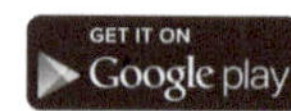

Available from all online music stores. Many albums are also available on Spotify and Pandora. Enjoy the music!

Jerald also presents to various music schools, groups, and associations throughout the country doing workshops, music camps, master classes, concerts and firesides to inspire and motivate teens, adults, music students and teachers. He enjoys teaching piano students about music theory, improvisation, and composition. He refers to himself as a Music Mentor and encourages music students to get motivated by music and to motivate others through music of their own.

Book Jerald as a Presenter/Performer for your next event:

Contact: Suzanne
jeraldsimon@musicmotivation.com
seminars@musicmotivation.com

Below is a list of some of the speaking and performing events Jerald has done and is willing to do.

We can customize to your specific needs.

Speaking and Performing at Events:

Workshops, Seminars, Music Camps, and Concerts (i.e. Concerts/Mini Concerts, Corporate Events/Parties/Dinners, Schools, Youth Groups, Recitals, MTNA Conventions and Conferences, MTNA Chapter Meetings, other Music Organizations, Schools, Groups, etc., Workshops, Summer Camps, Devotionals and Firesides, and any of the following:

Anniversaries, Awards Nights, Banquets, Birthday Parties, Children's Birthday Parties, Celebrations, Christmas Parties, Church Services, Clubs, Community Events, Conventions, Corporate Functions, Country Clubs, Cruise Ships, Dinner Dances, Festivals, Fund Raisers, Funerals, Graduation Parties, Grand Openings, Hotels, Jingles, Movie Sound tracks, Picnic, Private Parties, Proms, Resorts, Restaurants, Reunions, Showers, Studio Session, TV Sound tracks, Weddings, and customizable performances to meet your personal needs).

Book Jerald as the next Speaker/Entertainer for your next event! Motivate those who attend the event with Music Motivation®! Music Motivation® Workshops, Seminars, and Music Camps are focused on Theory Therapy, Innovative Improvisation, and Creative Composition with a Music Mentor. The emphasis is on teaching music students with "Music that excites, entertains, and educates". If you are interested in becoming a Music Motivation® Mentor, please email Music Motivation® at musicmentor@musicmotivation.com . If you would like to book Jerald Simon as the Music Mentor presenter or motivational speaker for your next event (i.e. recital, MTNA chapter meetings, workshops, summer camps, devotionals and firesides, corporate events, etc.) Please email Music Motivation®.

Booking Jerald is subject to his availability and waiting list.

I have various **"Cool Song"** packages available for all piano students and piano teachers on my website (musicmotivation.com) where students and teachers can purchase my music. Each of the "Cool Songs" are emailed to Music Motivation® mentees (piano teachers and piano students) according to their preferred music package. See which of the Cool Songs packages is the best fit for you and for your piano students (if you are a piano teacher) by visiting: http://musicmotivation.com/coolsongs. I also comes out with **Theory Tip Tuesday** instructional videos I share on youtube.com/jeraldsimon.

The "As If" Principle by Jerald Simon - $16.95 (154 pages - 222 poems)

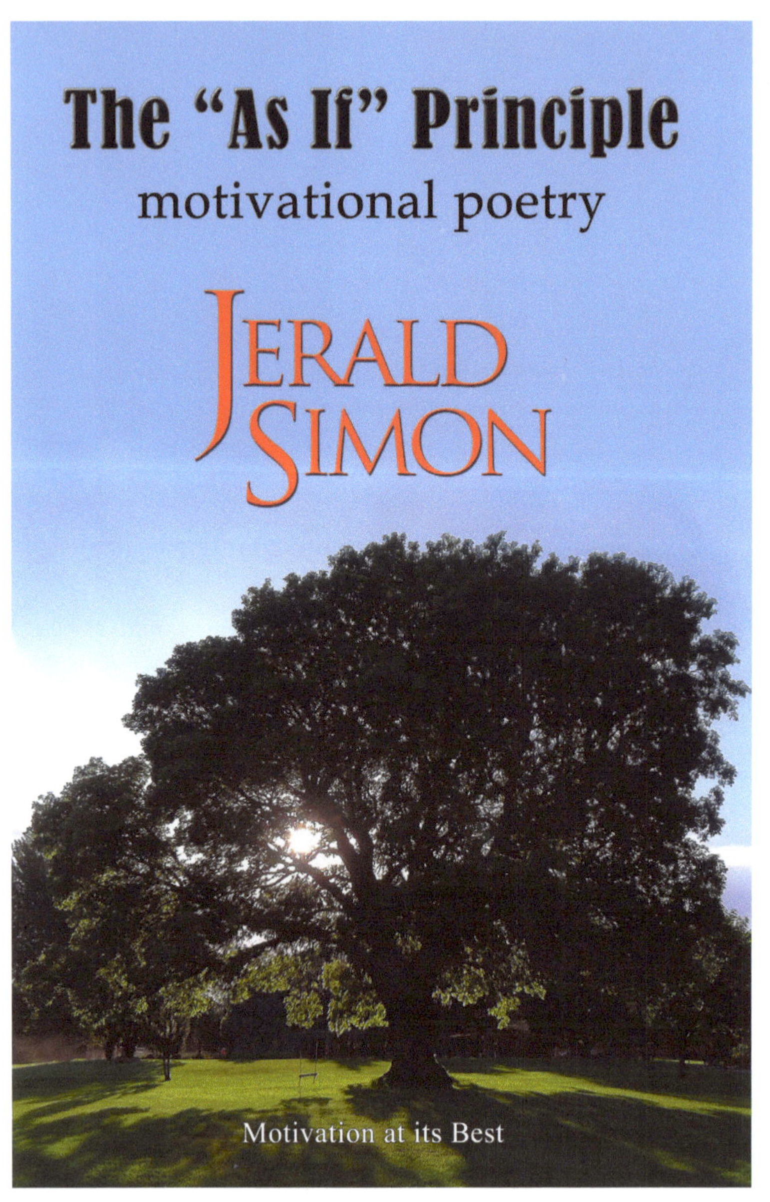

Other poetry books by **Jerald Simon**:

*** Poetry that Motivates * Poetry Smoetry * Season of Life**

The "As If" Principle (motivational poetry) by Jerald Simon features 222 original motivational poems written by Simon to inspire and motivate men, women, businesses, organizations, leaders, mentors, advisers, teachers, and students. The poems were written to teach values and encourage everyone everywhere to do and be their best.

The poems were written over a 20 year period and contain motivational advice about never giving up. It's about doing what it takes, believing in yourself and your own abilities and believing in others. The poems focus on such topics as:

Honor, courage, success, strength, will power, leadership, possibilities, confidence, goal setting, optimism, rising above mediocrity, character, never doubting ourselves, being productive, learning from adversity, doing what it takes, being happy, seeing the good in others, forgiving, seeing our own potential and the potential in others, learning life's lessons, righting wrongs, becoming a self starter, learning to control our thoughts, words, and deeds, and many more.

You can also purchase this paperback book on Amazon and also from Barnes and Noble. The audio book, where you can listen to me reading the entire book, is also available on i Tunes, Amazon, and all Online music stores.

Perceptions, Parables, and Pointers by Jerald Simon - $19.95 (216 pages)

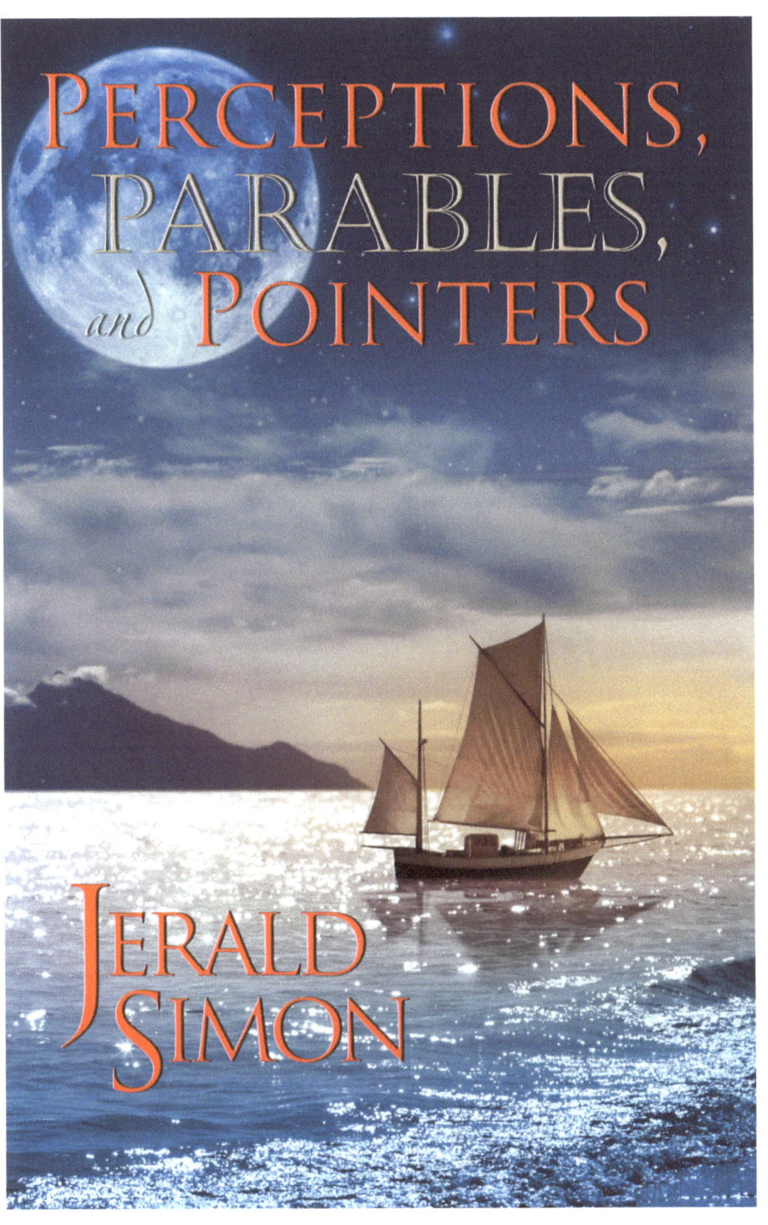

What do you really want to do with your time? What is your mission in life? Where have you been, and where would you like to go? What are your dreams, your hopes, your wishes? If you could do anything in the world, what would it be?

The main goal in writing down these perceptions, parables, and pointers, and in creating this book in general, is to present ideas that will help get people thinking, imagining, planning, creating, and actively participating in life.

Much of what has motivated me and pushed me forward in life is based on what I tell my children almost daily: "When we fall down, we GET BACK UP!" If you say the first part to my children, "When we fall down", they all automatically respond with WE GET BACK UP! This encompasses not only physical falls, but mental, emotional, spiritual, financial, and all different kinds of falls. This ideology began when I was eight years old and had fallen off of a 50 foot cliff. I cracked my head open and the doctors lodged a total of 26 staples in my scalp. I endured seizures for the next year, as well as frequent doctor visits, CAT scans, and MRIs. As a result of the fall, I have no memory of my life before the accident. It is a miracle I am alive and was not paralyzed. After my fall from the cliff, I resolved that each day would be a new birth for me regardless of how many times I would fall down, both literally and metaphorically.

You can also purchase the paperback book from Amazon and Barnes and Noble. The audio book, where you can listen to me reading the entire book, is also available on i Tunes, Amazon, and all online music stores.

Visit **musicmotivation.com/shop** to learn more.

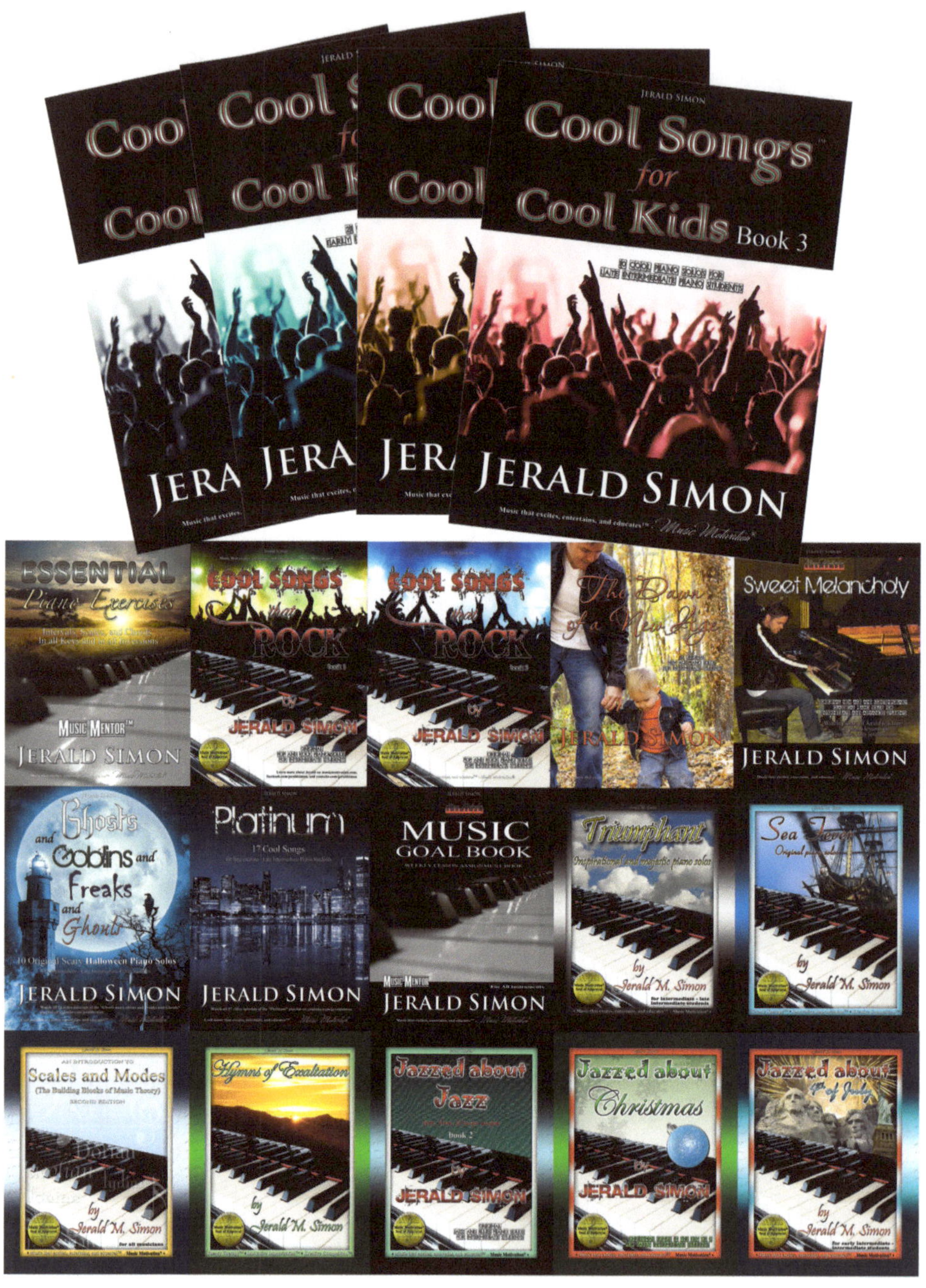

I have also created 21 music books of original piano solos - most with music backing tracks of other instruments and sounds. In total there are over 250 fun piano solos between the 21 books from pre-primer to advanced level pieces that have been composed primarily to motivate teenagers to play the piano!

www.ingramcontent.com/pod-product-compliance
Lightning Source LLC
LaVergne TN
LVHW070137110826
845147LV00002B/277